Covert Emotional Incest:

The Hidden Sexual Abuse

A STORY OF HOPE AND

HEALING

by

ADENA BANK LEES,
LCSW

ISBN 13: 978-1983999109
ISBN 10: 1983999105
CreateSpace Independent Publishing Platform
Tucson, Arizona

To Mom and Dad
and all the fond memories we
share.

WHAT OTHERS IN THE FIELD HAVE TO SAY

❧

"Using her own experience and her healing journey as a springboard to educate others, psychotherapist Adena Bank Lees teaches the reader how to identify and heal from this rather common, yet often not acknowledged, family dynamic. She addresses CEI's devastating impact on a child caught in this more subtle form of sexual abuse. Her easy-to-understand explanations of the consequences from her personal childhood trauma and her steps to recovery will enable readers to relate to her, to understand their own experiences better, and to learn how to get help for themselves. Also, very useful are the summaries in boxes in several chapters which clearly explain the main concepts of that chapter. I heartily recommend this book!!"

Jennifer Schneider, M.D., author of *Back from Betrayal: Recovering from the Trauma of Infidelity* and *Sex, Lies, & Forgiveness: Couples Speak on Healing from Sex Addiction.*

❧

"Adena Bank Lees guides us on a powerful and informative journey through her own experiences with *Covert Emotional Incest: The Hidden Sexual Abuse.* Not only does this book tell of her journey to healing but offers valuable information and resources that bring clarity and light to those who suffer from this form of trauma. Rarely is there a book that combines such a compelling story with clear and helpful strategies for recovery. I consider this a must-read for both clinicians and individuals who identify with this painful phenomenon."

Rokelle Lerner, Senior Advisor, Crossroads Centre Antigua. Author: *The Object of My Affection is in My Reflection: Coping with Narcissists.*

❧

"Adena Bank Lees' courageous new book, *Covert Emotional Incest: The Hidden Sexual Abuse,* is an important addition to the field of sexual victimization and psychological trauma for women and male survivors, their families, and psychotherapists. She has not only added a new term to the field, but exquisitely described it in easily understood words. Adena is courageous because she has chosen to tell her own story to help inspire the reader to fully comprehend the complex nature of CEI and its damaging after-effects. Through each step of the book, she shares significant insights to help each reader name what was done to them and to see how they still may be suffering. Adena shares key steps to healing and serves as a great role model and mentor to any survivor of CEI, who needs hope and a path forward."

Howard Fradkin, Ph.D. Author, *Joining Forces: Empowering Male Survivors to Thrive;* Business Partner, Collaborations Training, LLC.

"In this heart-centered and insightful book, Adena Bank Lees provides a close look at the psychological issues and challenges faced by individuals who have experienced covert forms of sexual abuse. This is a moving read, filled with stories of the author's personal journey in recognizing and moving beyond these harmful dynamics. It offers a step-by-step look at recovery, along with a trove of therapeutic explanations, professional wisdom, and guidelines for healing."

Wendy Maltz LCSW, DST, author of *The Sexual Healing Journey: A Guide for Survivors of Sexual Abuse.*

❧

"Adena Bank Lees' work, *Covert Emotional Incest: The Hidden Sexual Abuse*, is a tour de four that touches the heart and feeds the mind. As she shares her own story of covert emotional incest and her recovery, the reader is privileged to look into a window to moments of great angst, increasing awareness, and eventually healing. The true gift of her book is that is bridges that gap between a personal memoir and the passing of her wisdom onto others. This book serves as an important resource on this all-important topic, providing teachings that create an opportunity for personal and professional growth."

Kate Hudgins, Ph.D., TEP is the author of *PTSD Unites the World: Prevention, Intervention and Training in the Therapeutic Spiral Model* (2017), among many others.

꒰

"*Covert Emotional Incest: The Hidden Sexual Abuse* comes at the perfect socio-political time, educating professionals and the public about this unspoken and elusive form of sexual abuse. It is a must-read for mental health and substance abuse professionals due to the prevalence of this abuse in clinical practice. Ms. Lees clearly demonstrates and inspires the reader to make the key healing decision of *"I choose me"* rather than sacrifice their needs and boundaries for those of their parents and/or others."

Mary Kiernan-Tighe, LCSW. Private practice specializing in addictions and anxiety disorders.

꒰

"In her impassioned memoir, *Covert Emotional Incest: The Hidden Sexual Abuse,* Adena Bank Lees takes the reader through untangling the labyrinth of confusion, anger, and denial associated with covert incest. Many women will find this book as welcomed validation. *Covert Emotional Incest,* successfully adds to the growing recognition of the many forms of covert sexual abuse prevalent in our culture."

Kenneth M. Adams, Ph.D., CSAT-S. Author of *Silently Seduced: When Parents Make Their Children Partners* and *When He's Married to Mom: How to Help Mother-Enmeshed Men Open Their Hearts to True Love and Commitment.*

❧

"In my work with survivors of sexual abuse, I have seen over and over again the impact of overt sexual abuse. I have also seen the impact of covert emotional incest, but could not, until now, define this in a way that resonated with my clients and helped normalized their experience. Lees approaches the topic of CEI from a personal perspective while drawing on her expertise and training, making this book a practical guide with heart and soul. This should be a required text for any practitioner working with survivors of abuse.

Rachel Grant, MA, Sexual Abuse Recovery Coach.

CONTENTS

INTRODUCTION-PREFACE

Welcome! I have written this book to introduce you to the concept of Covert Emotional Incest (CEI). The following pages were born from a long-standing passion to offer a context for what you may have experienced. I thought I was crazy until somebody finally explained what was happening to me. This was such a relief and validated that I was not crazy after all! Therefore, I have used my story as a format for this book hoping that you would benefit, as I have, from hearing another person's personal experience. In particular, I share some essentials, how I coped, and what I have done and continue to do to heal. In addition, I have included teaching- boxes, which provide you with a more formal and in depth look at CEI.

Through this writing, I bring CEI out of the shadows and shine light on the process of identifying and healing from it. This light must be bright given how subtle, elusive, and normalized this family dynamic is in our society. The stories I have included illustrate how I identified, accepted, began, and continue to heal from the devastating impact of CEI. I share both painful and fond memories, along with how I came to develop compassion for my parents, giving this book a fullness that is not often provided in writings about abuse.

Four professionals, who were instrumental in my understanding of CEI, are Pia Mellody, RN, Pat Love, PhD, Kenneth Adams, PhD, and Wendy Maltz, LCSW, DST, all pioneers in the field of non-contact forms of sexual abuse. Rather than paraphrasing, I have quoted them directly to give you the base from which I started and eventually developed the concept of CEI.

Pia Mellody (1989) in her book, *Facing Codependence*, introduces Emotional Sexual Abuse:

> Emotional sexual abuse occurs when one parent has a relationship with a child that is more important to that parent than the relationship with the spouse...It is

sexually abusive because it creates a great deal of confusion about sexual identity, preferences for affection and direct sexual behavior. (p.169)

From *The Emotional Incest Syndrome: What to Do When a Parent's Love Rules Your Life,* Pat Love (1991) states:

When there is a high degree of enmeshment...it merits a special term: emotional incest...Children are powerless against an emotionally Invasive Parent. Adult children of emotional incest often have sexual dysfunction problems in love relationships. Often the children and adult children only see what they have gained from this relationship—praise and affection, extra privileges, patient tutoring, and shared confidences. (p. 8)

Ken Adams describes Covert Incest in his book, *Silently Seduced; When Parents Make Their Children Partners* (2011):

Covert Incest occurs when a child becomes the object of a parent's affection, love, passion, and preoccupation. The boundary between caring love and incestuous love is crossed when the relationship with the child exists to meet the needs of the parent rather than those of the child.

The child feels used and trapped... A psychological marriage between parent and child results; the child becomes the parent's surrogate spouse...sexual feelings and energy are never put into perspective. To the child, the parent's love feels more confining than freeing, more demanding than giving, and more intrusive than nurturing. The relationship becomes sexually energized and violating, even without the presence of sexual innuendos, sexual touch, or conscious sexual feelings on the part of the parent. (pp.15-16)

Wendy Maltz (private conversation 2015) distinguishes between covert and emotional incest—covert incest being the sexually charged words or behaviors toward the child. For example, a father may stare at his daughter while grabbing his wife's breasts, exclaiming, "Wow, these are luscious!" Another example is a parent coercing a child to watch pornography with her/him. Emotional Incest is when the child is made the surrogate spouse or confidant to one or both parents—the child is seduced on an emotional level.

While Pia Mellody speaks of Emotional Sexual Abuse, Pat Love uses Emotional Incest, Ken Adams calls the dynamic Covert Incest, and Wendy Maltz differentiates between the two. I offer you the term Covert Emotional Incest, CEI.

So then, what is Covert Emotional Incest and why did I expand the previous labels and definitions? Briefly stated, CEI is an elusive, *emotional* form of sexual abuse that occurs in the family system without there necessarily being direct genital contact. It is incestuous due to the undercurrent of sexual energy between a parent and a child. It is characterized by the following:

(1) triangulation; (2) breach of the intergenerational boundary; (3) surrogate, substitute spouse or confidant role; (4) objectification.

In CEI, the child may be exposed to highly

sexualized information and material. She/he experiences violations of personal boundaries such as hugs that are too tight, required kisses on the mouth, and/or her or his body being keenly focused upon. All this generates what I call the "cringe" factor. CEI is not limited to the opposite-sex parent-child relationship. It can also occur in the same-sex parent-child relationship. CEI is an equal opportunity destroyer. It insidiously attacks families from all walks of life, regardless of race, nationality, religion, socio- economic status, sexual orientation or any other characteristic. High risk families are those with one parent, mental or medical illness, addiction, and/or other stressors.

CEI also meets the criterion for Judith Herman's (1992) definition of psychological trauma: "…an affiliation of the powerless. At the moment of trauma, the victim is rendered helpless by overwhelming force. When the force is that of nature, we speak of disasters. When the force is that of other human beings, we speak of atrocities. Traumatic events overwhelm the ordinary systems of care that give people a sense of control, connection, and meaning."

The chapters of this book deal with issues such as the importance of *naming* CEI and exploring its effects on the person as a whole, then sexuality in particular. I also write about addictive behaviors, my search for the spiritual*, the significance of boundaries, and eventual forgiveness. They, like stories in life, are not necessarily told in a linear fashion. Some chapters combine written memories, comments, and professional teachings. In each chapter, my goal is to elucidate the symptom picture and web of entangled interactions stemming from the hidden and emotional nature of CEI. I also attempt to describe what is necessary for thriving rather than just surviving. Most importantly, a point I hope to make clear is that the relationships presented are definitely incestuous on an emotional level, with the resultant behaviors akin to those of persons who have suffered physical sexual abuse.

Over the years, I have heard from many that my teaching about CEI opened their eyes and changed their personal and professional lives and practice. Knowing the paucity of empirical research on non-physical forms of sexual abuse, my hope is that this book will be a catalyst for such action from the mental health community. I, personally, am committed to continue getting the word out about CEI through presentations, consultations, book readings, workshops, and trainings.

My healing journey was not a solitary one by any means. The combination of professional help, peer support system, and my parents' early involvement in treatment all worked together to bring me to this point. Yes, I was lucky to have parents who were open to listen and change, but I have also seen clients who are healing, despite parents who are missing, physically or emotionally. With all that I communicate, I wish to give others a sense of belonging, as well as hope that recovery and healing are possible.

I have lived a life of struggle, joy, connection, adventure and passion—and still do. I want to share specific elements of Covert Emotional Incest, but also be very clear that love, laughter, singing and dancing all happily coincided. Thank you for joining me on this journey.

Adena Bank Lees
January 2018

*When I use the term spiritual, I am talking about a connection to all that is, to a universal energy, such as that found in Nature. In my experience, persons who identify themselves as atheists are not exempt from these feelings of a need for connection. All persons can experience and heal from CEI.

THE MOMENT

I have been in individual, family and group therapy on and off since I was fourteen. It feels like one hundred years. Below I tell a story about one noteworthy session and its follow-up.

On this particular early spring day in 1989, I am now twenty-six and almost finished with graduate school—feeling pretty good about that. Yet, here I am, once again, walking into my therapist's office to speak about feeling so confused about the relationship with my parents, saying to myself, *"Enough already! When is this ever done?!? How many years to do I have to talk about this craziness! Am I blaming them or are the family dynamics really so messed up that they are the cause of such pain and confusion?"*

The sun is shining; it's a beautiful day, and I am talking and worrying myself into a hole again. Well, I do know that coming here has been helping me feel supported and I have gotten the strength to leave my current boyfriend Steve, certainly not the relationship for me. Thank God, I got away…

But I digress…

I am sitting in the waiting room. The same chairs, the same wall hangings, the same receptionist week after week. I have been waiting in this room prior to each session for over a year. I look around at the other people. *"What are their secrets? What are they working on? Are they as crazy as I feel inside? They appear pretty normal. But maybe so do I. I am always dressed well, presentable. Have to look good (want to look good?) "Have to look good…"* – definitely a message from my family of origin. *"It's how you look, not how you feel."* A joke in my family, but really true. Another unspoken rule. Lots of unspoken rules.

Anyway, Linda comes to get me. Her smile is always warm and her voice soft, yet commanding. She is a woman in her early fifties with grayish hair, glasses and a kind face. A trustworthy face. She follows behind me as we walk down the hall to her office. I enter and sit on the couch across from her desk and 'power chair' where she sits. My body is calm. Yet my mind is anticipating what will come out of my mouth—and hers. Linda welcomes me and asks how I am doing. My mouth is dry and seems disconnected from my brain. Not answering her question, I begin to use words I never had before. Specific descriptions of feelings, sensations and behaviors I couldn't (afraid to admit to myself) put words to previously. And then it is out:

"I don't know what it is, but I feel like I am having an affair with my father. It is yucky and I don't like it. This is the first time I have ever told anyone. It is scary for me to even say it out loud."

And my inner voice now starts its own monologue: *"Oh my god, you said this/it/whatever this is. Can you reel it back in? No, keep going; there's no stopping now."*

So Adena's voice continues, "And, my mother seems angry with me whenever I spend time with him alone. She is cold, curt and distant with me and irritable and short with my father. It is like there is this sexual energy between my father and me that I can't explain. He, to my knowledge, has never done anything to me, no direct genital-sexual contact. He never sexually abused me the way some of my friends' fathers and stepfathers did."

"Continue," she says.

"I know my dad never touched me inappropriately but it feels like we are having an affair. My mom is jealous and it feels really weird. When he kisses me, it is on the lips and I get a slimy feeling, energy running through my body. I want to cringe. I usually do, but stuff it far down into my gut. But, kissing on the lips is just how we do it in my family. There is no tongue or anything, but it still feels slimy. And, I feel like there is something wrong with me for feeling this way." *"Whew! A mouthful, a lungful. Now, breathe, Adena."* But Linda invites me to continue,

"Is there more?"

So it tumbles out: "Well, I am currently reading materials about sexual abuse. A good friend of mine is talking to me and to her therapist about her stepfather molesting her for years— intercourse—and I just keep thinking that must have happened to me, but I don't have any evidence or recollection. I have looked at the book, *Courage to Heal.* I have all the symptoms of a survivor—but no tangible experience. That's why I feel crazy. And, how could I think this of my father?"

My heart is beating out of my chest. I am so angry but can't allow myself to admit it. The shame and guilt are sticking to my ribs, covering them with a thick layer of gooey stuff that I can't get off, making me feel really hot, flushed. I want to run and hide in the corner to disappear. Be invisible. *"How dare you speak like this about your parent, you ungrateful and disloyal bitch!"* And, another part screams above the din, *"You need to say this. It is true. You need to be heard. Maybe she can help you."* My hot eyes tear up as I look towards Linda, searching for something.

But, I do not wait for a comment from her. I continue to speak in spite of the war inside. "I don't know what to do about this. Dad complains to me about Mom, his troubles with her weight and we brainstorm how to fix Mom. I try to fix it all and Dad always says he feels better after we talk. He tells me how much he appreciates me listening and that I have good ideas; that I am so mature for my age."

Again, to Linda, "I don't know why all this is coming out of me today, but it is."

I continue, "…How could she be jealous of me? It almost feels like there is a competition for my father's love and attention. She tells me that Dad listens to me, not her. I can feel her frustration with that. She also tells me how angry that makes her. Am I doing something wrong? Am I doing something to make my father like me more, listen to me more? I know my dad loves my mom. I see it and feel it. I don't want to be in the middle of them. It has felt like this all of my life."

And then Linda speaks, "Adena, did you ever hear the term Covert Incest?"

"No, why?"

"Because it fits everything you are saying today and the dynamic you have described since we have been working together. You were just more articulate about it today."

"Covert Incest? Wow! I am not crazy! This is called something?!?! Maybe there is hope for me yet," I say inside myself. What comes out is, "You mean I am not crazy?"

"Not in the least. You are not crazy. This is real and it is very difficult to describe when you are the child experiencing it," is the response. "Let me tell you a little more about this. Covert Incest is when a child is set up in a family to be the surrogate spouse or confidant of the mother, father, or both parents. You have talked about being your father's confidant; about his pain, anger and helplessness regarding his relationship with your mother. You have spoken about sensing your mother's competition with you for your father's attention and affection. Your sensing the 'yucky' feeling or sexual energy between you and your dad is classic here."

My breathing slows down. The energy that was running fast in my body now calms. The sticky shame and guilt melt a bit and slide off my ribs. The big thump I heard and felt in my gut, anchors me in my body, in the present moment. It is as if I am here for the first time. I see clearly. I see Linda clearly. I don't want to run, hide and disappear anymore. I finally have a term and context for what I have been experiencing all these years. *"She sees me! Linda really sees me! She can help me with this. I am not alone hanging out there in space by myself. If there is a name for this, then other people must have it too. This is another area where I felt like a misfit and maybe I am not! This is so big."* My thoughts ramble on, *"My story finally makes sense. I am okay. There is an explanation for why I do what I do and have done, and why I feel what I feel. Thank you so much!"*

I'm ready to leave the office on that high

note, but wait—there is a loaded word that is niggling my brain even more, pecking holes into my new-found acceptance. The air is let out and I deflate.

"Incest?! This is called incest," I ask/say to Linda. "I have a friend whose father incested her. He had intercourse with her many times. My dad never did that, at least not to my knowledge. I wonder now if I just don't remember it. Several of my friends had been physically sexually abused and didn't remember until recently. And then the memories flooded them. Some are still piecing together bits and fragments. Do you think my father physically sexually abused me?"

Linda, in her comforting voice, makes it all so clear. "I can't say. What I can say is that Covert Incest is enough for you to be experiencing confusion about this question, having relationship difficulties, and a history of substance abuse and eating disorders that are all a part of your story. Covert Incest survivors have very similar signs and symptoms as those who have been overtly (physically) incested or sexually abused."

As irrational as this may sound, after hearing that last piece from Linda, I feel so relieved that at least I had a label and wasn't crazy. Yet there is still a bit of nervousness in my gut. A fear that maybe I was like my friends, that I was a physical incest survivor and didn't know it yet. The sickening feeling begins to bubble up and instantly I started searching for a possible memory or memories. *"Stop! Stop,"* Adena's newfound calm calls out and I finally settle into what Linda said, "Covert Incest is enough!"

I leave the session excited and hopeful, with the proverbial skip in my step. The sun is still shining. There is new hope for me!

A couple of weeks passed in which Linda and I discussed having my parents come in for family therapy to confront this—to tell them what I have been experiencing and what I have discovered. My parents have always agreed to come into family therapy, so I expected them to this time as well. I called them and they consented to join us with no hesitation. Of course, I gave no commercial—didn't tell them what this session would be about. So, back to the story:

Even though Linda and I have rehearsed what I can say, I am still extremely nervous on the appointed day. My body is shaking. *"Am I really going to be able to say this to them? Am I really going to be able to confront this? I don't know if I can do it. But I know I have to do it. I must know if my father sexually abused me physically or not. I have to tell them that I have felt this sexual energy between us and that I don't know what to do with it. Oh God, I really don't feel brave enough to do this!!"*

But here I am, in the office with Linda, before my parents walk in to join us. She coaches me, reminding me she is there to start the session and will support me throughout. And, then...my parents enter. My mom sits toward the back of the room, facing the door; my dad to my left; Linda to my right and me with my back to the door. Since I'm facing my mother, I can see that her legs are crossed and her top leg is shaking rather quickly. I know this gesture to be her anxiety and fear. My father seems pretty calm, leaning forward to hear what Linda is saying. I am shaking in my own right, hoping no one can see. Mom's leg is pumping.

Linda gives me my cue. "Mom and Dad, I want to talk to you about something that is very hard for me. I am asking you to please listen until I am finished...Dad, I feel this sexual energy between us that I can't explain. It feels yucky. I am not sure. It feels like we have been having an affair. I am wondering if you sexually abused me when I was little." My mother's leg is going a mile a minute now. It's about all I can focus on. Her face is taut. Her pocketbook is on her lap and she looks as if she is about to jump up and run out of the room. I am so in tune with her energy it is scary—I want to run out of the room, too!

But, they both say at the same time, "No! of course not!" My dad says, "Adena, I would never touch you inappropriately. I would never hurt you. I didn't sexually abuse you." Mom says, "He never did anything to hurt you! He diapered you! How could you even think this?!"

Linda intervenes and begins to speak about Covert Incest. She explains why I might be afraid I was overtly abused, the symptoms of Covert Incest mirroring those of physical incest. She continued by pointing out that my struggle with anorexia and bulimia, perfectionism, and anxiety, is a common response to growing up in a family where this dynamic occurs. I start to float away...

What I remember is that the session ended with great tension amongst the three of us. We walked out in deafening silence. At first, Mom and Dad, slowly and awkwardly slipped through the door, then me, falling behind, watching my parents almost running to make their getaway. We did not speak for the next several days. Dead space. I felt as if the umbilical cord had been cut. It was harsh, irrevocable—no going back. My mind swirled with the question of physical sexual abuse. Relief, guilt, shame, and fear consumed me. The secret was out. What now? Will there be resolution? If so, how will it happen?

My mother called and asked if I would meet her for a walk on the beach. I thought this was a first step toward reconciliation. Even though Linda had been thorough in her explanation about my concern, Mom kept asking me why I thought my father might have sexually abused me physically. As is common in Covert Incest, this conversation was about meeting her needs not mine. I imagined that she was devastated at the possibility of her husband being capable of such a heinous act. I think, too, that she was so distressed and also wondering whether he did it or not, but did not want to say. So, again, no resolution. Just more questions and *my* needs not met.

It wasn't until weeks later that my father and I finally spoke. Eventually, we discussed what took place in the therapy session. Even though I continued to use Linda's phrase, "Covert Incest is onough," as a mantra, the unanswered question of physical or overt sexual abuse could not be quelled. So, Dad and I both could feel the tension in our talks. To lessen my anxiety and to get a little space from the issue and the dynamics, I kept limited contact and did not spend any time alone with him. I had not yet learned to set healthy boundaries; however, I can see now that restricting our interaction was exactly the first step in doing so.

I moved away that fall. When we spoke, conversations were brief, yet I didn't lose my need for a dad, my dad. I just wanted our relationship to be clean. I knew I loved him but I wanted to be the daughter, not his surrogate spouse or confidant. During our talks one night, he told me he would do anything to prove that he did not hurt or touch me in any way that was abusive. I told him there was nothing he could do. I thought of my friends who were abused and told by their parents that they weren't. I just had to make sure that I hadn't buried any memory or memories. So, I told my father that I needed time to explore this on my own. I can only imagine now how tense and anxious he must have been while I was doing this searching

Ultimately, I concluded that my father had not overtly sexually abused me. This realization came after almost another year of therapy focused on exploring this possibility. During a visit from my parents, I told them about my conclusion. I saw, heard and felt their giant sighs of relief. My mother exclaimed, "You see, I told you he didn't do it!" I had anticipated a reaction like this, given her apparent desperation that day on the beach, and her history of unintentional self-focus. I would have loved to have heard from her, "Adena, this year must have been so hard for you, too." I took a deep breath and said nothing.

My mother had no idea of her role in Covert Incest (now what I term CEI) for quite some time. But to be fair, it was only later that I, too, learned that my mother's regularly using me as a confidant regarding her anger, pain and frustration with my father was another part of this unwieldy and destructive story.

❀ ❀ ❀

"You know, Adena, your mother is your best friend."

I heard this from my mother on countless occasions but didn't have the words to describe the impact on me. I was about twelve years-old, the age a young girl looks to her mother for guidance and as a role-model, when I remember it first really hitting me. I had come in from playing outside and my mother looked a little downcast (depressed?). As I sat next to her on the sofa, she seemed to perk up and gave me a hug. Then in a much happier tone than her demeanor had just shown, she said, almost conspiratorially, "You know, Adena, your mother is your best friend. And I want you to be *my* best friend."

"WHOA! WAIT! WHERE DID THAT JUST COME FROM?!?!?
WHAT ABOUT ME?!?! WHAT DO I WANT?!

I did not want my mom to be my best friend. I did not want to hear about her frustrations with my father or how she wanted to divorce him. I wanted her to be my mom! I wanted her to shield me from this stuff! But, of course, I did not say anything. I was trained to do my job, which was to meet her needs. I did know that this felt yucky, too. If some sort of thermogram were done of my body at that time, I am sure it would have shown the turmoil and intensity of emotions that would be very similar to what I felt with my father—many of those emotions settling in my gut.

When I was around thirteen, she said it again. But this time I was empowered and 'teenage-enough' to have some words and I answered her with, "I don't want to be your best friend!" "Why not?" she asked. "Because I just don't. I have my own friends." I couldn't explain it any further. I still wasn't an adult with adult knowledge and perspective. I did not have a clue about this thing called Covert Incest. My body reacted how it had always responded to this statement—tense, ready to run, sick to my stomach, my head swimming in conflicting messages. How inappropriate her desire and voicing this desire was! How much it hurt, angered and confused me! I felt trapped—a theme that got imprinted somehow and would run throughout my life in intimate relationships.

❋ ❋ ❋

In recounting the above stories, an important point to stress is that Covert Emotional Incest, which encompasses Covert Incest, can occur just as easily with the same-sex parent as well as with the opposite-sex parent. Since it does not appear as 'sexual', it can be even more of a conundrum. And, since this is the parent that I got my own sexual identity and self-concept from, I believe it might have had more of a deleterious effect on my burgeoning sexuality and self-perception. My relationship with my mother, her weight problem, and her keen focus on my physical appearance affected my entire body image. I often felt like an object—a thing, created to please her and others, rather than a human being in my own right. Being told to go on a diet at eight years of age embedded the message of, "You're fat! and if you are fat, no- one will ever love you!" into my brain. All of this contributed to the development of anorexia, depression, and perfectionism.

Adena, as a fourteen-year-old anorexic →

The dynamics of CEI have continued to manifest periodically over the years. I see that my recovery entails having consistent boundaries and, just as important, acceptance of my parents for who they are. As always, this is a work in progress.

There are four major concepts relayed in this story that are important to understand.

- The family as a *system*
- The *intergenerational boundary*
- *Triangulation*
- *Objectification*

It is generally accepted in the mental health community that a family operates as a *system* in which each person plays an interactive role. Healthy families have what is called an *intergenerational boundary* in place. The intergenerational boundary is an invisible structure or energy field that defines the power differential between parent and child. It is flexible, not rigid or diffuse. This structure dictates the natural consequences of behaviors and determines the appropriate interaction with the child on both spoken and unspoken levels. In essence, this means that the parent is responsible to meet the child's needs, not vice versa. Likewise, the child has a voice in the family, yet does not have the final say regarding decisions that affect the family.

If the boundary is rigid, the child has no say in the workings of the family. If it is diffuse, the child may meet the parent's needs as surrogate spouse (with or without overt sexuality). They may also make adult decisions and can emotionally hijack the household. Part of constructing the intergenerational boundary is having parents or caregivers participate as a 'unified executive committee' to maintain the framework that ensures the child's safety and well-being. Ideally, in a single parent family, she/he enlists assistance and support from external sources in order to sustain and enforce this boundary.

A metaphor often used in the field to represent a family system is that of a child's mobile hanging overhead. When the child reaches up and pulls on one of the parts, it causes the mobile to go out of balance. Stress in a family is like a child pulling on one of the pieces of the mobile; it too creates an imbalance. What we know about systems is that they strive for homeostasis, another word for balance. Marital problems, addiction, serious medical/mental health issues, and being a single parent, are just a few examples of these stressors. Without asking for outside help, the family relies on itself and adapts but its balance is precarious.

One adaptation to this imbalance is a dynamic called *triangulation*. This is a set up for CEI. Triangulation happens when major caregivers, not possessing the skills necessary to deal directly with each other, may use their child as an intermediary. In CEI, this manifests as the child meeting the parent or caregiver's individual emotional and/or romantic needs. The system has therefore employed triangulation to balance and function, incorporating destructive and abusive behavior patterns.

Objectification is another component of CEI. The child is *used*, not having their feelings or needs as, considered. The Cambridge Dictionary describes it as, "Treating people like tools or toys, as if they had no feelings, opinions, or rights of their own." Sexual objectification, more specifically, according to Wikipedia, is, "The act of treating a person as an instrument of sexual pleasure." Pornography is a prime and glaring example of objectification. Yet, the subtle role interplay of Covert Emotional Incest fits these two descriptions exactly.

Sexuality - Sensuality

Sexuality and sensuality are crucially important topics for anyone who has suffered the trauma of overt or covert incest and abuse. In this chapter, I am practicing boundaries—the boundary of not over-disclosing. The details of my sexual life remain private. I will, instead, share a few stories to demonstrate the points I wish to make and the information I wish to impart. First, I want to lay out what sexuality and sensuality are for me. Then I share with you how CEI impacted my beliefs and behaviors. Finally, I illustrate what sexuality and sensuality have come to mean after years of hard work in psychotherapy, 12-Step programs, and real-life experience.

For the purposes of this book, *sexuality* includes the following:

- Gender role definition: What does it mean to be a woman?
- Sexual orientation: What gender(s) are you sexually attracted to?

- Sexual fantasies: The mental and sensory representations of what arouses you.
- Sexual behaviors: The actions you take to express your sexual interest in, lust for, or your love for another. E.g. flirting, passionate kissing, oral sex, etc.
- Sexual beliefs: Ideas you have been taught (directly or indirectly) and/or conclusions you have made from behaviors you have been the object of, or witnessed. This also includes societal norms and the view(s) you hold based on contemplation and critical thinking.

Sensuality is a perception of sensations resulting from something that happens to or comes into contact with your body. It does NOT have to be touch of a sexual nature. For example, temperature of the air, type of shower you like (hot/cold, pulsing water vs. stream), smell and feel of a beautiful flower, and the sound of a mourning dove calling its mate outside your window. Sensuality, however, is present in the best sexual experiences.

Below I share a series of questions/issues concerning my sexuality and history of CEI. My hope is that they are helpful to anyone struggling with their own.

How did CEI inform my gender-role definition?

What did CEI teach me about being a woman and what it means to be a woman? Amongst other things, it taught me that women are recipients of male sexual intrusion and intimidation, including unwanted touch or comments.

It also taught me that I am supposed to like these advances and be flattered by them as opposed to being angry and offended. Saying "No" was never an option. I learned that a woman is only worth something if she is sexually attractive to a man and provides him with what he desires. CEI taught me that a woman is only attractive to a man if she has the perfect body and dresses provocatively. And, who defined the perfect body? My father. He deemed both voluptuous women and almost anorexic women to be sexy. Very confusing, to say the least. This objectifying attitude towards women was puzzling and contradictory because I was also taught to be strong, have my own mind and opinions, and to defend myself when necessary. I stood up for myself in many ways, but regarding sex and love, I was impotent—no pun intended. CEI had its way with me in this arena and the following story is an example of the mixed messages I received.

It was a sunny, warm fall day. My father and I were driving upstate to visit my grandmother. I was fifteen and quite despairing because I had not yet had a boyfriend. Since I had a history of unrequited love or crushes since I was a little girl, it reinforced my CEI training to interpret this as my being worthless and unlovable. As we got out of the car, about to go into my grandmother's apartment, the question I had been painfully pondering came out. "Dad, why don't boys like me?" This was a genuine question of a daughter to a father. It did not carry the yucky feedings or inner conflict that CEI conversations were filled with. "Adena, you are a strong and powerful young woman.

Boys your age, and even many men, for that matter, are afraid of a strong woman. There are boys and men who are not afraid, but they aren't common." I loved my father so much in that moment. He told me the truth. I knew it. I could feel it deep inside. There was a break in the CEI cloud. I so appreciated our honesty and ability to speak to each other this way. He continued, "You are not an ingenue. That is what most males in our culture are looking for. You stay true to who you are. The man who will celebrate your strength is out there. Be patient."

Wow! Why didn't I have a father
like that?!?! Oh wait, I did!

In becoming a mature woman, I am clearer on what is true for me instead of what CEI or society taught me about what it means to be me. It is true for me today that being a woman means I am worthy just because I exist. I do not need to be physically attractive to a man, please him, or anyone else. I have learned that a woman holds her vulnerability as her strength. For example, I no longer equate sensitivity, innocence, and a soft heart with being a victim. These are strengths as much as independence is. As neurobiological research has proved, a woman is hard-wired for connection and it is natural for her to seek out genuine relationships.

As a woman, I want these and, yet, am entitled to set limits. "No" means "No"—no explanations, no excuses. "No" is a complete sentence. As a woman, my body is to be celebrated and respected since it is the vehicle in which my soul lives. Taking good care of my body is *my* job. I have the right to choose what I do with it—no one else owns, can touch, or comment on it without my permission. It is appropriate for me to be angry and use my voice when these boundaries are violated. I no longer blame myself, but hold the perpetrator accountable.

How did CEI inform/impact my sexual orientation?

While I'm not here to talk about gender fluidity or orientation on a continuum, I will discuss my views that have been hard-won from experiences over a long period of time. My conviction is that my sexual orientation was genetically set at birth. Therefore, CEI did not have an impact.

My orientation is to men of traditional western culture and to fairly androgynous women. What I do know is that CEI trained me to believe that sexual attraction to and from men, older men in particular, would buy me validation and worth, so I was solely with men for many years. It was only after I came into more personal power as an adult that I permitted myself to acknowledge my attraction to women. I no longer needed a man to approve of me. What I found, however, is that the indoctrination of CEI followed me into these new relationships. Yet now, because of my personal growth work, I no longer expect or rely on another person for affirmation of my sexuality or who I am as a whole. That is a job for me and my Higher Power.

How did CEI inform my sexual fantasies?

As has been stated several times before, CEI dictated that my personal value should come from men's sexual attention and my pleasing them. Therefore, my past fantasies were always about how sexual liaisons would provide confirmation of my being desirable and lovable. They were a way to escape the intense shame I carried that told me, "I am unlovable;" "I am not enough."

Today, my fantasies consist of passionate adventures. They are predicated on empowerment and self-acceptance.

How did CEI inform my sensuality, sexual beliefs and behaviors?

I often heard from my parents throughout my growing up years, "Making love is something you share with someone you love. You need to be mature enough to handle it." Unfortunately, due to the CEI dynamic, my self-perception was skewed in terms of how mature I really was. Remember, I had heard all my life, "You are so mature for your age. How do you know so much, you are so young!" So, it is not surprising that when I fell in love with my first boyfriend, Marshall, at fifteen, those words rang loud and clear. They led me to think, *"I love him AND I am mature enough to handle it.*

The following vignette is a clear example of the confusion stemming from a CEI dynamic invading my sexual identity and boundaries.

Over a salad and coffee one afternoon, my mother asked, "Is Marshall a good lover?"

"What are you talking about?", I replied, aghast she was asking me this, yet I knew what she meant. There was a way my mother always knew what I was doing. I got away with very little.

"I mean, is he a good lover? Does he kiss well? I know you have had intercourse with him. I know you, Adena. You are in love with him so I know you have slept with him."

Appalled, I gasped inside myself, *"Eww, gross! Do you want to share him, Mom? Are you trying to live vicariously through me? Why do you want to know this? You are NOT my friend and even my friends don't ask me things like that!"*

Again, I was shocked and angry that she was invading my private life, my very private sex life. *Her* perverse need, not mine, and there was no way I wanted to or was going to talk to my mother about this!

My body tensed and I spoke in an angry and defensive tone, "I am not going to answer you, Mom. It is none of your business." Thank goodness for the natural impulse of separation and struggle with one's parents during adolescence. I was setting a boundary without even knowing that word or concept.

My mother asked this question a few more times during the several months I was dating Marshall. I never answered. She inquired about other partners I had had over the years as well. I never answered. I think my father knew better than to ask.

It was after the breakup with my second, high school boyfriend that promiscuity became the norm for me. Feeling that deep hole inside and not having other tools to fill it, I relied on the illusion of power taught to me by CEI. This illusion felt good, but it was an illusion, nonetheless. The experiences were demeaning. The beliefs and consequences were:

- First, I am responsible for a male's erection. If I can get him aroused and sexually engaged, I am also responsible if he abuses me.

- Second, if I can attain the conquest, then the emptiness, powerlessness, and helplessness I feel from the inability to stop the confusing messages and energy inherent in CEI (as well as the physical sexual abuse I endured) would go away.

- But, as soon as I would have sex, there was no filling of the hole inside nor erasure of powerlessness and helplessness.

- On the contrary, many encounters replayed violating experiences, which just reinforced this dysfunctional cycle. This is called reenactment (see below).

In addition to the sexual aspect of relationship, CEI strongly impacted my ability to have intimate romantic relationships—"mating" problems, as Wendy Maltz, LCSW, DST, calls them (personal conversation, 2015). My mother never liked who I dated. My father was more reserved with his opinion. There was often a struggle of loyalty for me, between my partner and my parents. I admit that this continues and is something I am constantly negotiating.

As stereotypes would have it, my parents' desire, especially my mother's, was for me to marry a nice, rich, Jewish doctor. This need of hers was so strong, that she set me up with someone she thought met this profile. Unfortunately, he was not that nice. He raped me on our first date. Because I thought there was something wrong with me that I didn't like him, I went out on another two dates with him. My mother's indoctrination seized my brain, *"There couldn't be something wrong with him, how could there be, when he was Jewish and studying to be a brain surgeon?"* The last was a double date with a dear friend of mine who said, "He and his cohort are total creeps! I am never seeing them again!"

My friend didn't know this at the time, but she gave me permission to be free of the hold my mother's wishes had on me. Her evaluation and exclamation affirmed what I knew to be true but could not admit to myself, for I was afraid of being traitorous to my mother and her needs.

This man, and several others I dated were many years my senior. My involvement with older men stemmed from my CEI struggle. I was reenacting the relationship with my father. One man I had an affair with was twenty-five years older than me. Talk about Freudian!

In longer term, more serious relationships, I found myself choosing significant others who distanced themselves sexually after the 'honeymoon', usually about six months later. I made this about me and was terribly obsessed, sad, and desperate. High anxiety and neediness became the norm, versus the emotional strength and independence I knew I had in me—and that these men fell for in the first place. Unfortunately, my partners carried their own sexual baggage into the relationship. This made for much hurt, shame, anger and, again, confusion.

A significant aspect of my healing has been to develop compassion for my younger self/selves. According to Richard Schwartz, Ph.D. (1997), we all have such parts. I can say now that I feel sad for those child, adolescent, and young adult parts of me. They were lost. Time and again, these parts would put themselves into situations where they were used, coerced or forced to do things they did not want to. They were searching for love, worth, and a filling of the hole inside that was created by CEI.

"Watch this from the ceiling. It is safe up here. You don't want to be down there in your body. It is way too painful and scary. Just perform, focus on pleasing him, and all will be well," said a young part of me.

I have come to understand that this behavior meant I was dissociating during the experience, a strategy that survivors use to protect themselves. This part did save me during dangerous encounters, but with those whom I loved and was safe, it robbed me of feeling or sensing the good. *(Young selves who have experienced trauma cannot discriminate between the past and the present. They should not be present in a sexual encounter. See teaching-box below for a definition of dissociation and parts of self.)* I often missed out on sharing the special emotional, physical and spiritual connection with my significant other that sexual intimacy is meant for. I had no awareness of choice regarding this dissociation. There were times I willed myself to be present but it was unpredictable.

Truly honoring and embodying my sensuality and sexuality has been a process. It has taken many psychotherapy sessions, 12- Step work and, simply put, practice to be where I am today. It started with identifying emotions and the physical sensations that accompany them. The next step was to pay attention to the sensations I liked most. After that, I was able to identify those I did not like. Staying in my body with these sensations was difficult, needing a lot of support. Breathing deeply played a big role in my success. Currently, I have boundaries, empowering me to say "No" when touch or other sensations do not feel right and/or are not warranted. In fact, I felt it necessary in this book to write a chapter on boundaries, because they are the first and most affected casualty of CEI.

I am now, and have been, for the past seventeen years, monogamous with a partner who celebrates me and lays no shame in anything sensual or sexual. She has provided the safe space to explore and embody the beauty that is me. I get to experience a special emotional, physical and spiritual connection I have longed for and that is my birthright. Finally, I have been released from the prison of sexual beliefs and behaviors caused by CEI.

In my clinical practice, I have seen clients enjoy this type of sexual connection with others, no matter where they are or the other is on the sexual gender continuum. It is about the person you choose, not their gender identity.

SOME NOTES ON THIS CHAPTER

PARTS OF SELF

According to the Internal Family Systems Model of psychotherapy developed by Richard Schwartz, Ph.D. (1997), we all have parts of ourselves that work together in our internal and external world in order to function. Certain parts are created to deal specifically with the pain of abuse and/or unmet needs of the child. These parts end up taking on roles such as caretaker and fixer in order to deal with and

---

manage this pain. Their purpose is to protect and aid in survival even though their behaviors may lead to harm self and others.

<h2 style="text-align:center">DISSOCIATION</h2>

Dissociation can be one of the coping mechanisms developed to deal with the overwhelming feelings caused by traumatic experiences. Mental Health America defines dissociation as "...a mental process that causes a lack of connection in a person's thoughts, memory and sense of identity." (MentalHealthAmerica.net).

Dissociation seems to fall on a continuum of severity. Mild dissociation would be like daydreaming, getting 'lost' in a book, or when you are driving down a familiar stretch of road and realize that you do not remember the last several miles. A severe and more chronic form of dissociation is seen in the disorder Dissociative Identity Disorder, once called Multiple Personality Disorder.

Dissociation and other dissociative

disorders can lead to an experience of feeling detached from the environment, people nearby, or the body.

REENACTMENT

"Reenactment is a process that includes compulsively repeated thoughts, attitudes, and patterns of behavior. The goal of reenactment is to resolve and heal a past traumatic experience or series of experiences. Reenactment arises out of our past and can seriously disrupt our present lives and relationships."

(http://www.bernsteininstitute.com/traumatic-reenactment/).

It is mainly an unconscious process that rarely leads to mastery of an event, or the event's associated feelings and beliefs. However, there are instances in which we can consciously choose to re-enact a past trauma to integrate and work through it. The expressive arts therapies (psychodrama, art therapy, music, dance, etc.) are excellent venues for this type of reenactment.

However, the critical feature here is for

the work to be done safely and with full consciousness. A wounded child/person is never expected to correct a hurtful experience on their own, which can only be done with knowing support by the therapist or other group members. The key is to reconstruct the old situation in a new way, creating a healing moment.

An example of this is a woman who was sexually abused as a child and who, as a result, was terrified of physical contact. She began massage therapy training, placing herself in a situation reminiscent of her past trauma. Exploring her massage therapy experiences in psychotherapy enabled her to work through her overwhelming feelings and beliefs related to her sexual abuse and diminished her fear of physical contact (Parkes & Weiss, 1983). This story is retold in an extensive article in which the psychological makeup, behaviors, and compulsions of persons who have suffered trauma are described along with suggestions for therapy. (Levy,1998)

Relocation ... Transformation

In 1990 I was lucky enough to get a job at a premier addiction and trauma treatment center, the best of its kind at that time. So, with little trepidation, I moved from New York to the Southwest. I just thank God for the 12-Step programs with their built-in backing, allowing me the comfort to know that I would meet people and build a support system quickly.

I needed to leave New York—partly for the independence from my parents, a serious physical boundary that I thought would aid in my healing from CEI, and partly because of the Long Island Expressway! I just couldn't do the 'parking lot' of daily traffic any longer. I also knew I could not make enough of a living on a social worker's salary to ever afford a house, etc. I had had a dream of living in Marin County, California since I was a young teenager and wanted to move west. I knew that area was unaffordable at this time, but, knowing a little of geography, I thought this move would be my first hop toward the coast. However, in this move to the Southwest I discovered at least two things: Yes, there was no traffic, but no matter, whether you are physically near parents or twenty-six hundred miles away, the effects and dynamics of CEI travel with you. I had made this important boundary and separation from my mother and father, yet I entered another world with its own problems—another dysfunctional family.

In my interview, the man who would be my superior described the working environment as "family." Oh, how did he know I wanted so badly to have a healthy family—one who shared my language and my commitment to personal growth? My inner being was rejoicing, feeling warm and safe, singing, *"Here are professionals, all in recovery. They must be healthy. Finally, I get to be in a functional family! Yay!"*

Well, in a short while I found all this turned out to be quite the fantasy, my dreams and hopes dashed once again. What I did not know until later—about five months or so—was that this was a 'good ole boys club' of active sex addicts and narcissists. Yes, women worked there, but the management was mostly men and there were many male therapists, most of whom were older than me—I was twenty-eight at the time. I was being sexualized by these men and spoken about behind my back, in closed-door staff meetings and gatherings that I wasn't privy to. How did I find this out?

Early on, the Program Director, my boss's boss—the one who hired me and told me this was a "family"—came to my office and, without any preface, said, "I need to make a 9th Step amends to you. I have been talking about you in a sexual manner and sexualizing you with other male staff." I froze. My heart pounded and yet I could not move a muscle. I was flabbergasted, shocked, and didn't know what to say. I did not expect this; in fact, it was the last thing I ever expected. This man was supposed to be in recovery, care about me, and protect me from stuff like this! Boy, was I naïve. It was a re-enactment of so much of my childhood CEI. I trusted an older man and men, only to have them sexualize and betray me. Betray me in an emotionally sexual way, with no physical touch—just as before. So, in my frozen state, I didn't know what to do but to say, "Thank you for telling me."

I also wasn't fully aware at that moment that this was an 'emotional rape'. His 'apology' was selfish and self-centered, about him soothing his own conscience. Confessing to me was a victimization in itself. He didn't care about me—in his act of contrition he cared only for himself. So, this self-important and self-centered man, in appeasing his own guilt, re-traumatized me. Why am I emphasizing this? Well, my historic reactions — minimization and confusion — reappeared, shutting me down. It doesn't matter that he apologized because he felt bad. What matters is the impact on me — re-traumatization, this woman's experience of male violence. This level of experienced re-traumatization can get lost with CEI, with my internal voice saying, *"He never touched you and he feels bad. Just let it go. What is the big deal?"* Well, again, the big deal is that this was abusive and I was re- traumatized, pure and simple. It is exactly the reason I'm writing this book. The effects of CEI are devastating; they are not less because the abuse is covert or unintended.

It would take some time for me to identify the subsequent rage that I suppressed at this incident. So, I sat stunned and quiet because I feared losing my job and did not have the words or concept of sexual harassment (this was before sexual harassment was widely recognized as abuse). And, being where I was in my own healing from CEI and the shame I felt, I didn't tell anyone about this until I left the job years later.

There are two important pieces I add here that are asides to the chronology of my story. The first is about the qualifications of the 9th Step. The 12-Step originators in their wisdom, knew that this step of making amends could be used to appease one's own guilt, so they added the caveat, "...except when to do so would injure them (*victim*) or others."

The second is that sexual harassment breeds shame and fear even with women and men who do not have a CEI or overt sexual abuse background. This initial sexualizing of me and this kind of subversive behavior from someone who is a superior is all about power—it is not about sex—and it yields the same type of feelings of powerlessness, shame, guilt, even horror at being used.

Re-enactment can lead to the same fight-flight-freeze response as occurred in the original trauma. Being overwhelmed by the experience, the left brain goes dim, while the right brain and amygdala are screaming, *"Danger! Something's wrong!"* The left brain, in the meantime, is struggling to make sense of what is going on, so it roots around in the file cabinet of memories and tries to piece together a story. What comes up are often disjointed images, physical reactions and sensations, and an incomplete story, with blame being placed on the wrong person, the one being abused.

All the while, the 'victim' might appear calm and composed, not an accurate representation of what is really happening internally.

The abuse continued a few months later in a supervision session. My immediate boss, from behind his desk blurted out, "I can't stop looking and thinking about your breasts." *(I was wearing a black maxi dress with a scoop neck that did not show any cleavage—as if what I was wearing even mattered!).* Again, I immediately froze; got nauseous, needed to flee. I got out of there as quickly as possible, ran to my office, shut the door and called my sponsor (a mentor in the 12-Step program). At least in my paralysis, I knew to do this. I saw my boss as a big brother and thought he was safe. In the few months I had worked for him, he did not ever say anything to me or do anything sexual. Here was an older man who did not see or treat me as an object, or so I thought. I did not want to/could not believe he would do this.

Looking back, I see now that denial kept me from the awareness that he was probably one of the staff with whom the program director was sexualizing me. I was sobbing and shaking on the phone with my sponsor. I wanted to run out of the building and never return. Like many times before, I felt tremendous shame and fear. I was confused about whether this was my fault. Part of me knew I had done nothing to ask for this comment/behavior, and part of me still believed the training I had had: *"You, a woman, are so powerful that you caused and are responsible for his arousal."* This was a double- edged sword for me and clearly depicted what I had heard years earlier—that 'powerful and powerless' are connected: Powerful to make men sexually defenseless yet powerless to stop the victimization. Once again, I was as helpless as a little child.

My sponsor did help, reminding me that I did not have control over my boss's behavior. She continued, emphasizing that my power really came in focusing on calming my body and reminding myself that it was not my fault. There were other examples of harassment—probably more than I've remembered—but this next one brings the shame I had experienced out into the open.

I was having lunch with the clinical staff of about ten therapists and one of the males said, "Adena, I want you to know that the men on staff have been objectifying and talking about you in a sexual manner for a long time." I was mortified. In front of all my peers! This particular guy said he did not partake in the comments and that he confronted the others and wanted me to know. My body got hot. The urge to crawl under a rock or chair or anything, just not to be seen, was overwhelming. The shame was unbearable. I was victimized and violated all over again. No one touched me but I was stripped naked. I felt so slimed, as if they ran their dirty hands all over my body and were peeping at me too. Yuck! The same experience I had most of my childhood. When will this stop?! I kept my composure because that is what I do. But inside I was screaming and wanted to yell out, *"Do you want an award for telling me this? Do you get a special 'thank you' for not being part of the 'gang rape'? Telling this story in front of the group—why didn't you come to me personally and show real care?"*

These occurrences took me and my body

back to earlier experiences in my life. I froze, I was sexualized, I was confused, I was an object—exactly how I felt being a victim of CEI. It still amazes me that I questioned my own legitimate feelings of rage and anger. Yet, the above internal words were questions and observations I would never say, could never say back then. So, I was left with the despairing feeling that here was another male I could no longer trust.

Within seven months of employment at the treatment center, the combination of sexual harassment, betrayal (by my bosses and other male staff), and my own perfectionism brought me to my knees and I eventually relapsed into bulimic behavior and suicidal depression. However, before writing about my inpatient stay below, it is important to note that the stories I relate are essentially universal and, with name and some specific detail changes, can be the stories of so many overtly and covertly abused people.

They are metaphoric in some ways and if we extract their essence we can see that there is a causal relationship between the CEI people have experienced and certain behaviors. In my own case, there is a clear connection between CEI and the maladaptive behaviors and situations I found myself in—ranging from eating disorders, substance abuse, sexual objectification and inappropriate behavior, to not knowing how to set boundaries and, subsequently, pervasive and suicidal depression.

While things continued to devolve at the addiction center where I was working, healthy recovery messages began to seep into the cracks in my thinking, into the battered parts of my soul. Periodically, a special phrase like "Easy does it," etc., or event would have significance and I would feel lightened and enlightened, but one time is not enough. Soon my resolve would erode and all good intentions evaporated without my even realizing that I was once more on that slippery slope into my destructive behaviors.

The decline was subtle—in fact, I thought I was doing a great job. After all, I was working up to fifteen hours a day documenting client notes perfectly by spending exorbitant amounts of time dictating to get them just right. My notes were so good that they were used by the center when the credentialing body came in to audit. I got kudos for this. But at what cost? So, there I was—the perfect therapist, the perfect treatment plan creator, the perfect documenter, just as I was the perfect daughter. I didn't know how to do it any differently. Yes, the patients were getting a good therapist, but one who was falling apart on the inside. I turned to my old friend, the behavior I knew would help me get through—bulimia. It is clear now that the bulimia helped express the rage, shame, guilt, loneliness and powerlessness that I was feeling. Nothing in my repertoire could supplant this self-destructive pattern. And yet, something must have been there because in my suicidal hopelessness, I knew/remembered one thing from the 12-Step program—to ask for help.

So, I went to my clinical supervisor and begged to go to inpatient treatment. She stood by me. When I told my immediate boss (the one who told me he couldn't stop thinking about and looking at my breasts), he insisted that I only would need a five-day intensive. Again, I thank God that I could stand my ground with the support of my clinical supervisor and the full thirty-five-day treatment protocol was approved. I was in the center from mid-October to the beginning of December 1990, spending my twenty-eighth birthday and Thanksgiving there. It was a new birth and I give thanks for that.

Below is a short recap of our family therapy sessions. They are important to note because the lessons I and my family learned can be valuable to all who have family relationship issues.

I am sitting in the group room, this first day of family week, surrounded by my mother, father, brother, seven primary group members, and another group member's family. This almost-boulder is lying in my lap—a ten- or more-pounder, off white, holes all over, both rough and smooth in places. I was rubbing my hands and fingers over it. Caressing it as if it were my new born infant. Nurturing it and at the same time it was my support. My lifeline.

A week prior, my primary counselor, Margaret, gave me the assignment to carry this large rock wherever I went. It represented my need to control. The goal was for me to feel its heaviness, physically and concretely, and the consequences of this need regarding people, places, and things—basically, everything around me and inside me. I felt out of control most of my life. Carrying the rock was inconvenient and annoying, but in a way, it felt comforting. It was my safety; I knew it. Control, or the illusion of it, was how I organized my world so that I could cope. With it I could function, work, have friends, stay thin, sober, etc.

In the session, my dad is sitting at the edge of his chair, leaning forward, his hand cupping his left ear most of the time because he can't hear the family therapist speaking. (He is losing his hearing and won't get a hearing aid. Selective hearing— an example of his way to manipulate and control.) I am angry watching him continue to ask the therapist to repeat himself.

I don't remember a lot of details or specifics of the group after that. What I do remember, and remember distinctly is what happened the next morning in primary group.

My therapist declared, "Adena, your family is the most controlling family I have ever seen in the twenty-eight years I have been a therapist. You need that rock and I want you to keep it as a shield throughout this week of family therapy."

Internally I exclaim, *"Whew!"* followed by a big sigh of relief. My heart slows down and my muscles relax. My mind silently rambles, *"I am not crazy! Thank you so much, Margaret, for validating me! This is just like when my therapist Linda told me about Covert Incest. Yay!"* "Okay, thanks," is what actually comes out of my mouth.

Two days later, while in group again, I am literally shaking with fear and anger sitting face-to-face with my father. I want him to feel MY experience of his behavior. I hope that revealing these secrets in front of the group will allow him to 'get it' and take ownership of his insensitivity. I am providing specific examples of CEI here. How can he deny it? Others will see and hear this too. I will be validated, finally!

I have the paper with the five items, that I had prepared very carefully, in my lap for reference. Items listing moments when I felt I had been abused. Items that start with, "When you say/said, do, etc....I feel/felt..." I want to say it all with respect and I am determined to be present with my anger, which is, in effect, respecting myself. It feels good and right.

Dad and Mom were instructed to just listen and not respond. I begin:

- "Dad, when I was fifteen with my friends in the living room and you walked by on your way to the kitchen with only your underwear on, I felt ashamed and angry."

- "Dad, when I told you how I felt about this and you responded with, 'It is your fucking problem,' I felt ashamed, angry, and scared."

- "Dad, when you confide in me about

your problems with Mom, I feel special, yet scared, overwhelmed, confused, and angry."

My father's face is non-moving, his eyes wide. He seems very surprised that all this has come out, but I have no idea what is going on underneath. And, since I'm being true to myself, my dad's feelings don't matter to me right now. I'm feeling empowered and there's a bit of, *"Ha, I got you, Dad. Everyone now knows!"*

My mother is now asked to sit and face me. The empowerment stays with me as I sit up straight, take a deep breath, and look down at my paper to state the first item. My hands are trembling.

- "Mom, when you confide in me about your problems with Dad I feel special, yet scared, overwhelmed, confused and angry."

- "Mom, when you want and expect me to be your best friend, I feel angry and trapped."

- "Mom, when you so keenly focus on

what my body looks like, I feel ashamed, confused and angry. I feel like an object rather than your daughter."

My mother's face is one of horror. I cannot help but be impacted. I am beginning to wilt and find myself leaning in to take her hands, but my empowered self shows up. *"Stop right there! Her feelings are not your job to fix. She is an adult and can deal with them herself. She has the support of her group and the family therapist. YOU ARE NOT HER THERAPIST!"* I sit back in my chair and remind myself to breathe.

The group ends. I am surrounded by hugs and the verbal support of my primary group members. I feel a hundred pounds lighter. There is a freedom inside that I have never had before, however, it is not yet complete.

The next day, I am in the group room again. It is my turn to sit and listen. My stomach is turning, awaiting what I will hear. My feet are planted on the floor and I am ready to keep as much of a poker face as possible. To just sit there and take it. I can break down afterwards in the arms of my primary group members. A part of me is hoping my parents really 'give it to me' as I have seen with other families. Another part of me wishes for it all to be over before it even starts. My father begins:

- "Adena, when you told us you were suicidal I felt and I feel great fear."

- "Adena, when you invited us here for family week I felt and feel grateful."

The family therapist then asks, "Do you have any other concerns to share with Adena?"

"No," says my father.

My internal voice: *"That's it?!? I feel cheated! Did you forget the rest? Did you not see all the stuff I did and went through as a kid/adolescent? Any feelings about my anorexia? You were there when I got diagnosed! How about drinking? You saw me falling down drunk. I can't believe this! Oh well, I guess I have to accept that you are not going to say anything else."*

Now, I turn to my mother. I am listening intently. She shares the same concerns and nothing more. When it's my brother's turn, he does the same. I am disappointed that the only confrontations I received were about me wanting to end my life. I was ready to hear real tough ones from them since I had seen many confrontations prior where families let it all hang out.

It hits me hard, however—the word 'suicide'. There is something in hearing them say it and say it in front of the group that gets my heart. Like a punch. *"Wow, this is really true. This is what I was honestly contemplating."* The seriousness of it becomes real for the first time. I feel guilty and sad that I caused the three people, whom I love the most, this level of pain and to have that much concern for me. I have empathy for them given the heartache I can see on their faces. I don't want to hurt them. I never wanted to hurt them.

I have to say, though, that I feel seen—

as if I matter in a way that I had never felt before. They cared that I lived or died. Of course, I knew they did, but this was somehow different. It was right out there— tangible. The reality is profound.

To be fair, "I was jealous. I can still get jealous," did come out of my mother's mouth during the last day of family therapy. This happened when the word "affair" was again used to describe my father's and my relationship. Her owning of this jealousy was another big validation. Again, I was not crazy. By the end of the week my parents had held themselves accountable for their covert and emotional incestuous behaviors. We had learned more about boundaries and had begun implementing a few. The roles of surrogate spouse, hero/rescuer, and perfect child were identified, and their negative impact and contribution to suicidal ideation and self-destructive behavior was acknowledged. We had now established a central thread of understanding that was woven into, and throughout, our lives up to the present. This is not a fairy tale, however. Our family has remained far from perfect. I am constantly reminded of the phrase, "progress not perfection."

The whole treatment experience was an enormous turning point, saving my life and transforming my family's life. I was able to have a relationship with my parents and brother because of it. I would have had to cut off contact with my parents for some time if it weren't for the education they received and the forum for direct and brutally honest communication that the staff provided. The structure of the process and the skill of the professionals cannot be ignored and it informed my personal way of dealing with my own clients later. And, to give honor where honor is due, I greatly respect my parents and brother for being open to much of what was presented to them. A telling statement from my psychologist father at the end of family therapy: "I learned more in five days than I did in getting two Master's degrees."

My story is not every CEI story. I have treated many adult clients whose family members are deceased, not willing to participate in family therapy, or for whom the relationship is too toxic. This does not mean these clients do not get a chance to heal. What it does mean is that we identify other methods through which they can confront and set limits. Writing a letter comprised of the "When you, do, say, etc., ...I feel..." statements and reading them in the therapy office is a perfect example.

Because I am a certified practitioner in experiential psychotherapy (psychodrama), I have facilitated many clients reading their letters to a group member playing the role of their parent, or imagining their parent in an empty chair. This works because the brain does not know the difference between actually confronting the person and doing it in a role-play situation. If this is handled correctly, similar feelings and results can be experienced, so it is always important to speak with your therapist about alternative ways of addressing CEI.

GROOM...BOND...BETRAY

It was the next to the last day in family therapy at inpatient treatment. The story continues:

Having just finished work with my brother, Scott, who is three years older than I, a wave of emotion hits me and I lean over in my chair sobbing, "Jerry abused me! He sexually abused me!" There is a hush in the room. It is intensely quiet. I think I am crying for at least two- three minutes. The waves of feeling keep coming and it is hard to breathe. The sobs continue. When the waves subside, my body and mind experience incredible relief. A secret that I did not even know I was carrying has been released and my mind clears. I am still vulnerable, however, as I peek to see my family's reactions. "I'll kill him! What did he do to you?!" comes from my brother.

Shame creeps in again, my inner voice frightened, *"Am I exaggerating?!?! Jerry didn't penetrate or overtly fondle me as a child. Will Scott dismiss what happened? Not believe it was sexual abuse?"* I, myself, begin to minimize my revelation even though, just a few minutes prior, it was undoubtedly real.

Jerry had repeatedly asked another boy, Bobby two years younger, and me to come over to his house to play hide and seek. Jerry was sixteen and I was eleven. Because he was my brother's friend and so much older, I felt as if I were special. *"He wants to be with and play with me? Wow! I am not a misfit."* I did not get how absolutely inappropriate and weird it was for a boy in eleventh grade to want *to play* with a fifth and third grader. Of course, I had always wanted to hang out with my big brother and his friends. I looked up to them and, if they welcomed me, it verified that I was cool and older than my years.

Looking back on this game we played, I can see that Jerry made sure that he and I hid together in cramped spaces. Bobby's job was to do the counting and seeking. Facing each other, Jerry held my body close against his. I could hear and feel his hot breath. I could sometimes feel a hard thing in his pants, but did not know what this was. All I knew was that it felt yucky, scary, and good at the same time. The contact was too close and for too long—similar to the hugs and kisses on the mouth accepted and normalized in my family but with more fear attached.

Telling this story to my family, the shame enveloped me like a heavy wet blanket. And the feelings mirrored my internal experience of CEI— the conflict between knowing something was wrong and some of it feeling good. I had been coerced and yet felt privileged.

I told the details of Jerry's abuse for the first time in the above setting. My sobs were so guttural and wrenching, because I had realized the true horror and betrayal—Jerry had used, groomed, and sexually exploited me. I had never before thought that what he did to me, and later as an adolescent and young adult, was sexual abuse. I did not know I was caught in a trauma/betrayal bond. I believed I was making a conscious choice and that I had the power to have consensual sex with him as an adolescent and young adult. But, again, just as in CEI, I was trained to believe I was powerful and adult-like.

BETRAYAL BONDS

Throughout the literature and in this chapter, the words that repeat are exploitation, power and betrayal. This is because CEI and overt sexual abuse are NOT about sex; they are about the misuse of power, which *is* exploitation and betrayal of trust. So, before continuing with the Jerry story, I would like to insert some words about a pernicious effect of CEI— trauma/betrayal bonding. According to Patrick Carnes, Ph.D. (1997), betrayal bonding, as he calls it, affects the mind and psyche of a child and adolescent, with these attachments causing a "...distrust of your own judgement, distortion of your own realities, and the placing of yourself at even greater risk." (p. xvi).

He uses the term betrayal bond because he believes it speaks more directly than trauma bond to the dynamic and the feeling people experience, as well as the fact that a fundamental betrayal does take place in the relationship with the abuser. He states that a "…betrayal bond is an attachment…with a person who is dangerous and exploitative…of incredible intensity or importance, or both…whose signs include misplaced loyalty, inability to detach and self- destructive denial." (p. xviii).

It is known that people who come from dysfunctional families, in which there was abuse or trauma, are particularly vulnerable to seduction. When a person feels flawed and unlovable, flattery, attention and kindness can further disarm any resolve or concerns and the person will ignore an inner voice whispering, *"Don't do this."* Carnes emphasizes that "Anybody can be seduced, but if a person is shameful, needy and afraid, they are much more easily led down the trail of exploitation." (p. 54)

CEI is a pattern of something that occurs daily. It activates the nervous system and fortifies distorted beliefs. CEI sets up the formation of betrayal bonds by:

- Training you to *not* trust your intuition.

The abuser and others challenge your perception of reality, so that you are confused about what is real or right or fair.

- Persuading you to give over your power to someone else because their love and attention is what is most important for your survival.

- Indoctrinating the belief that your worth and lovability are tied to your sexual attractiveness, overriding the fact that the behavior is abusive. If the person does not validate your sexual attractiveness, you revert to shame and the fear that something is wrong with you. You push them for a sexual response or any form of attention. This becomes an addictive obsession and compulsion in that you are powerless on your own to stop it. Like all addictions, this need for sexual attention becomes primary in your life and other things fall to the wayside. CEI can also create an opposite experience—denying sexual needs or "sexual anorexia," as Carnes calls it in *Sexual Anorexia.* (1997)

CEI, in and of itself, is an exploitative relationship and a betrayal of trust and power. The brain organizes to see this exploitation as a way to get needs met and decrees what is "normal" so that judgment is impaired.

Betrayal bonds and the way we cope with trauma can form life-long patterns in our relationships. Some signs are loyalty to people who have betrayed you; consistent attraction to untrustworthy people; secrecy, minimizing or normalizing the exploitation or abuse; continued contact with the abuser who acknowledges no responsibility; the inability to say, "No. No more!"

As with any addiction, the only way to break the bond is to deal with it directly. I have found that path to include:

- Identify it as such—an addiction and a betrayal bond.
- Feel the feelings of betrayal.
- Mourn the loss and losses.
- Set and enforce firm and consistent boundaries. (See Boundaries chapter for

details.)

- Surround yourself with supportive people.
- Begin forming healthy, secure, life-affirming attachments.
- Forgive yourself. (See Face of Forgiveness chapter.)

It is important to note that in any traumatic relationship an unspoken contract of sorts develops between the perpetrator and the victim, yielding a loyalty that makes no logical sense. But if this is examined closer, it becomes clear that the loyalty results from the person's identity being so tied up with the relationship. The more fear and shame in the relationship, it seems the stronger the bond, the stronger the loyalty. In cases of extreme abuse, the person's life may be reliant upon the relationship, therefore confronting the perpetrator or a precipitous breaking of the bond can create suicidal thoughts, and indeed, suicide.

Breaking these bonds takes more than personal strength and willpower. Just as with any addiction, healthy support is necessary. When the 'victim' can develop an identity that is no longer based on abusive and destructive patterns, it becomes easier to make the final break with the perpetrator and subsequent trauma bonding. (Hudgins & Toscani, 2013)

Jerry and the betrayal bond with him were woven throughout my developmental years and beyond. He escorted me and my friends, as early as age fourteen, to concerts, allowed us to hang out with him and his friends, even his girlfriend. He presented himself as sensitive, kind, and paid a lot of attention to me. He showed and told me I was important to him. I found myself liking Jerry more and more—wanting and almost needing to be with him. Yes, there was always a part of me whispering, *"What is Jerry doing hanging out with someone so much younger? He has a girlfriend. This isn't right."* But, as is common with betrayal bonding, I dismissed my doubts and instincts.

Eventually, under the influence of this betrayal bond, having lost my ability to have sound judgement, I 'agreed' to have sex with Jerry when I was sixteen. I find it interesting now how he calculated, hovered, and waited so that no one could say that it was sexual abuse. Predators groom their victims who are always less powerful, by making them feel special, important, and chosen. My parents, through CEI, groomed me too, but the abuse was covert and unconscious. They had no intention of hurting or abusing me, while it appears that Jerry certainly had in his mind for years that I would be his prey.

So, it happened in his bedroom of his parents' house. Jerry told me that he and his girlfriend had an open relationship and that I was the only one he would be sexual with other than her. He said he had felt strongly about me for a long time. I do not think he actually ever said he loved me, but that is what I heard because one of the things CEI taught me was to equate sexual attention and energy with love. I was not in love with him but could not stay away from him. There was this pull and I did not know what it was. As I write this now, the tears flow because it is still so painful. If I could go back in time, I would run to rescue my young self. Essentially, I would be the good parent and tell her that her instincts were correct—what Jerry did was wrong, emphasizing that what happened was not her fault.

The night of his engagement, I was eighteen. He came to my house and informed me of the news. I congratulated him; I was genuinely happy for him. His engagement allayed some of my fears and guilt, since I thought this would be the end of our physical relationship. But…"Let's celebrate by having sex," he said. "No way!" I exclaimed. A moment of clarity descended upon me—I saw through the trance of the betrayal bond. This was now a moral boundary—no more physical relationship once there is engagement or marriage. He pouted and then got cross, angry, his eyes small and piercing, "Why not? I told you we have an open relationship and this is perfectly fine!" "Because you are engaged. That makes a difference for me. No more." I stated. "Oh, I can't believe you. If that is the way you want it, fine," and he walked out.

Yes, I was able to say, "No," however, the betrayal bond was still active in its power to keep me silent—I never told anyone this last part of the story until writing this book. I saw and spoke with Jerry sporadically over the next few years, keeping up with him by checking with my brother. Even though I assessed him as a cheater and adulterer, I could not stop being involved in some way. I could not walk away. I was still bound by some need, by some pull. I was invited to and attended his wedding.

As I entered adulthood my resolve to stop being physical with Jerry did not last and the sex continued on and off through my mid-twenties. Despite my having boyfriends, graduating college, and working in my chosen profession, Jerry continued to be a magnet. I could not stay away— my compulsion to be with him overwhelmed my resolve. The might of the betrayal bond prevailed. I was now twenty-three and minutes after having sex, Jerry's wife walked into the house. Mortified, I once again awoke from the trance and realized what was happening. My inner voice spoke the truth with clarity, *"This is so not okay with me. It is outside of my values system."* I called Jerry shortly after this incident, telling him that I was done and it was over. In true narcissistic-abuser form, he accepted no responsibility and yelled, "You selfish bitch! You are the only one I will ever be with besides my wife. I do not go outside my marriage with anyone else. How can you do this to me?!"

Perhaps it was my new, budding sense of identity that allowed me to hold firm and hang up the phone. Unfortunately, a few months later, the betrayal bond seized me again because, as Carnes says, I had not yet dealt with this relationship "directly". My compulsion to connect with Jerry returned, so I called and asked if we could be friends. This time, he said a definite and permanent "No". I was stunned. The contact with him stopped, but not the contract. It would not be over for me until I resolved it in therapy.

Over the years, I have often thought about Scott's awareness of my 'playing' with Jerry and his apparent lack of concern while I was growing up. Scott did not seem to have a problem or question that his sixteen-year-old friend played with his eleven-year-old sister and later hung out with her as if she were a peer. He never said anything about it. Shortly after I had had sex with

Jerry, at sixteen, I told Scott. He was angry and I now realize that I told him hoping he would rescue me, and make sure it stopped. He obviously thought I was old enough to have consensual sex and held me responsible for it, despite it being statutory rape in New York State.

Only in retrospect do I question how all this could have gone unnoticed. Did alarm bells go off for my brother? Did he tell my parents? Did my parents know on their own that I was going over there? I cannot remember if they knew or not. If they did not know, why not? If they did and took no action, it was a gross failing on their part. Looking at this situation, skewed through the CEI lens, maybe they all thought Adena was 'mature' enough to handle it, so it was not a problem. In their eyes, she was not a little girl who needed to be protected.

Jerry sent my brother a touching email about memories of my father when he heard my dad had died back in 2015. When Scott told me about this, what came out of my mouth was, "He does have the sensitive and caring part of him that I remember." Was I still idealizing him—a residual of CEI and betrayal or trauma bonding? Or was I simply able to acknowledge a part of him that is really there?

It is challenging to explain the level of entrapment of the betrayal bond and its relationship to CEI. Unless one has had personal experience with CEI, it is difficult to give its power credence. This would be especially so with parents or siblings acknowledging the abusive qualities in a situation such as the one I had with Jerry. After all, in most persons' minds, I was old enough to make my choice. They would not understand that, because of CEI and the betrayal bond, it was not possible for me to have given informed consent, no matter my age.

As a result of all the years of therapy, study, and experience, I am now confident that I was Jerry's victim. Blaming the victim is a classic, patriarchal response. I posit that, we, who have suffered CEI, sexual assault, and harassment, have been indoctrinated to believe that victimization is our fault as well.

BOUNDARIES

When I began to set boundaries, my parents called me "hostile". They told me they felt hurt and unloved. As I see it now, enmeshment was my family's way of expressing love. Boundaries were translated into meaning distance and disengagement. Therefore, I was the 'bad guy', hurting them whenever I said "No" in some way. On the other hand, I was learning in psychotherapy and 12-Step programs that healthy boundaries allowed for true intimacy (in- to-me-see). This new knowledge liberated me, permitting me to say "No" without feeling guilty. It took time, but I was determined to no longer be held hostage by guilt. I worked diligently to say "No" to and release myself from the surrogate spouse, caretaker and mediator roles. This included getting support from peers, professionals, and much prayer and meditation. It was difficult, but I knew it was a necessity if I was to heal and have the quality relationships I so greatly desired.

Effective boundary-setting is a major first step in climbing out of the morass that is CEI. Putting up a wall, an impenetrable defense, was what I had thought of as a boundary. However, what I learned from Pia Mellody (1989) is that boundaries are something different. While sometimes a wall is required, boundaries are flexible and permeable. They can be emotional, physical, and/or sexual. They give us a way to embody our sense of who we are. A healthy boundary has tensile strength and allows a flow of energy. I get to choose whether a wall or a boundary is warranted, what I let through my boundaries, and with whom I set them. I also have a choice about the quality of the boundaries—how firm, deep, and strict. I can see through a boundary. My heart is visible, and I let the other person see me and my heart as well. They just can't reach in without my permission and grab at it. Boundaries provide a safe space to experience my sensitivity and vulnerability without shutting down.

As any novice, I started out sloppy, but I began to monitor what my actions and reactions were to the perceived breaching of a boundary. I noticed that I 'froze', losing my voice and ability to act in some cases. In others I became angry, often sounding indignant. On occasion, I would flee and get out of the situation as quickly as I could—a smart move when there is imminent danger. I also often questioned whether the breach was my fault. Did I do something to warrant this? Make this happen? Give the other person permission to violate my boundary? When I learned about the "fight, flight, freeze" response to fear, and how we can blame ourselves, my reactions made sense. Getting reality checks from my support system provided ongoing clarity about breaches as well as what my part was, if any.

Coming to understand that to have a truly intimate relationship there must be some boundaries, has been a life saver, really a 'self' saver. That is, to connect, I must have a 'self' and allow the other person the same dignity. For all the romantic notions that are flying around, it is not "we become one." It is the "I, the thou" (Buber, 1923) and the we—three separate entities. Two halves do not make a whole, yet the 'we' is the magic made by two wholes coming together. I've come to believe that a Power greater than either of us alone is in the 'we'. This Power is greater than the sum of its parts and manifests itself when in the 'we'.

Setting and enforcing limits has inevitably been a key ingredient in my healing from CEI, which, as has been stated, is the epitome of a boundary violation. Thus, in my recovery, I have continued to determine, refine and implement these limits. It is imperative that I remember that my role of daughter and my parents' roles of parents must always define our relationship. It will never be justifiable for them to confide in me about the other, objectify me, or use me as a surrogate spouse in any other way.

Self-esteem, as I was told, was required to set boundaries. That left me in a predicament—if I had waited until I had enough self-esteem to set a boundary, I would never have begun. But, at some point I became aware that I was looking at the concept of self-esteem wrong. It is not a one-time, absolute state of being. The fact that I was already seeking help meant that at least a flicker of self-esteem had caught hold in my psyche. So, I had to do it (set the limit) and, as I did, my self-esteem grew into a real flame. I was acting into new ways of thinking and feeling rather than trying to think and feel different before I did something different.

Things will not change until they begin to change. I was fully committed to and wanted healthier relationships, so I practiced this new behavior of setting and enforcing boundaries. The equation I still follow that has worked so well for me is:

awareness + different behavior/action

= different result.

And, yes, I got a different result. This book, this story I share with you, is about the mountain I have climbed to reach a happier, more sane life. I really could not have planned what has happened. To my delight, my relationships have been transformed. Because of my knowledge of CEI and the boundaries I have learned to set to take care of myself, I have seen that my 'self' is worth taking care of!

Here I relate several vignettes that illustrate my boundary-setting over time. I show you the full emotional picture to maximize your appreciation of the difficulty and triumph this behavior entails. The following story is my first attempt to extricate myself from entanglement (collusion) in the surrogate-spouse role.

I am twenty-seven. My body is vibrating, head swirling in thoughts. I'm revved up, feeling very young and, at the same time, moving into my power. "Mom, Dad, I can't talk to you about each other anymore. It is making me sick. Please stop doing this. If you attempt to draw me into collusion against the other, I will need to end the conversation and will call you back another time."

"Ok, we will try, but you may have to remind us," is the reply. Out loud I say nothing but am seething inside. A twisting in my gut and a voice yelling, *"Is it still my responsibility? Why don't you take responsibility? Again, you do not hear me or take my needs into account. Just say, 'Yes, of course. We understand. We won't do it anymore.'"*

Still shaking at my core, I hang up the

phone and call my best friend. "I can't believe what I just did. I set the biggest boundary of my life!" My heart is pounding out of my chest and, as my friend listens and supports me, my body calms and my mind quiets. Taking a deep breath and a sigh of relief, I notice that my feet are firmly planted on the floor. *"Thank you, Mother Earth, for providing the solid foundation I need."*

I don't know if my parents were aware of my tremors, but it really didn't matter. This was the first time I had set a limit as an adult—no shouting, sarcasm, or rebellion; a calm, firm, and steady voice. I did this with the encouragement and guidance of my therapist, Linda. She suggested the boundary based on what we had discussed and the impact the CEI dynamic had on me. She taught me that the anger I was feeling has a gift— the energy to activate self- care behaviors. Seeing anger in this positive light allowed me to set the limit with my parents, and frankly, to continue to do so.

I also learned to 'book-end' my boundary-setting by calling someone before and after I did it—brief and debrief. Relying on knowledge from 12-Step programs, I recognized my own human limitations and brought a Higher Power onto the scene, asking in silent prayer, *"Please put the words into my mouth."*

But, even deeper than the anger from the conversation with my parents, was an amorphous anxiety, a clouded, shrouded figure haunting me. I realized I had been avoiding this figure for a long time but now was able to see through the fog and named it as the dread of altering or losing the relationship. For good or bad, they were my parents and this relationship was so important for and to me. But with each boundary I set, the fear of losing the relationship confronted me and I chose to walk through it as thoughts tumbled in my head:

> *"Would they love me? What were we going to talk about? Do we have anything to talk about? How will I feel close to my mother and father if I am not in the caretaker, surrogate-spouse, listener, and mediator*

roles?"

Along with the anxiety and resolve I felt, I was beset by guilt. A sharp pain in my heart and loud voices in my head, all shouting at once:

"How can you do this to them? You are hurting them. What are they going to do without you? You are a terrible daughter. Being a daughter means listening to and taking care of them—not abandoning them."

I had no answers. The only thing I was clear about was that *I had* to get out of these roles. They were killing me, and something had to change. No, *I* had to change. Yet, it was nerve-wracking as I ventured into foreign territory, since, as I had learned, it was my responsibility to enforce the boundary, not my parents'. Even with all that internal confusion, there must have been some profound sense of confidence. So, I climbed up onto the high dive, held my nose and took the plunge into the deep waters of the unknown.

It happened this way: When I would end the first conversations without talking about the other parent—or me being in the middle, playing the old roles—part of me was elated, part of me was grateful, and part of me was sad. There was grief that the relationship was being redesigned and parts of me missed the *illusion* of intimacy or closeness, no matter how dysfunctional. It was a loss, so I allowed myself to feel its pain, not judge, have compassion for myself, and, yet, to continue on the path of change anyway. What I found emerging in our relationship were the beginnings of an intimacy that felt cleaner. I no longer had angst and the torn quality that I had had playing the old, familiar roles. This was a monumental victory. I removed myself from the surrogate-spouse role. I had transformed it to the appropriate daughter-parent one and established the intergenerational boundary.

As is always so with new behavior, the urge to fall back into dysfunctional patterns was pulling me. I found myself wanting to talk about my mother with my father and about my father with my mother. I noticed the impulse and literally swallowed hard so that I would not say anything at all. Having a set of behaviors to insert helped: Swallowing hard, making sure my lips stayed shut, changing the subject, were all options that I had been offered and they worked.

This is called containment—being aware of and holding my feelings and impulses, which is different than shutting them off or down. You see, in my family growing up, there was often no containment—you said what you thought, and you acted on impulse regardless of the impact on others. This lack of restraint was considered closeness and health. Yet, these behaviors were a paradox because I acted impulsively and said things spontaneously, but there was also so much I pushed down, did not say, and did not do.

Patience and time are essential elements in the process of change. Even with practicing new behaviors and increased awareness, it still took time to modify our old habits—my parents worked on their part as I worked on mine. In trying something new, a person usually sways from one end of the pendulum to the other and then finds the middle. I believe this is what my parents and I did. We did not do it perfectly, but continued making the effort and there was progress.

Related to the above story is a situation that

happened at the close of family week during my inpatient treatment stay, when I declared, "I formally resign from the family social worker role." My parents and brother were startled, yet expressed their respect for this boundary. The image of 'formal resignation' that this statement conjured up was something that I had felt empowered to do earlier in my life—me, walking into my boss's office and laying down my resignation letter on her desk, turning on my heels, and walking out. This scene appeared and stiffened my spine each time I spoke with my parents until I no longer needed it.

❄ ❄ ❄

"It's my divorce too!"

Another wailing, emotional comment that came from my mother's sense of loss at the dashing of her hopes for my first marriage to Charles. This jarred me because she spoke of the dashing of *her* hopes. This also conjured up the same feeling I had had my entire life of being invaded, as if she were plugging into me, trying to be me. The feeling was intense. I cringed with an impulse to back away and also push her away. I felt as if my mother was an alien taking over my body, my mind, my emotions.

Why was I surprised? Again, it had happened all my life. Because of her narcissism she saw me as an extension of her. Yet, I continued to believe this 'invasion' could not be occurring. The boundary struggle to reclaim my physical and emotional body went on for many years, but is now mostly resolved. Perhaps, it's resolved within me so that I don't get triggered by her unconscious emotional eruptions anymore—at least, not much.

❀ ❀ ❀

"It is her or me!"

This statement/ultimatum came from my mother during a very strained and emotional conversation we had about my marriage to my partner, Diane. As open minded as my mother thought she was, she drew the line with accepting my relationship, especially when we chose to marry. So, as she and I went round- and-round on this issue, my mother finally said in resignation,

"Well, I guess if I don't accept it then I am going to lose you and my grandson." My level-headed, unemotional response, of which I am proud, was, "If that is your choice, then yes. Look, Mom, I am not choosing you or her. I am choosing me." It was never discussed again.

❀ ❀ ❀

"My body is none of your business!"

This is a recent cry from me, so yes, CEI still continues. We had talked in family week about the keen focus on my body and how this was improper, painful, and disturbing. In the chapter, *The Face of Forgiveness*, I tell a poignant story about how, in an almost comical moment, my mother and I were showering together recently and the comments on my body did not materialize. It was a eureka moment, giving me so much relief. However, this issue has waxed and waned over the years and about a year ago, I just couldn't tolerate it as my mother was making comments about my body and appearance. I said, very firmly, "My body is none of your business! Stop talking and commenting on it!"

Of course, she defended herself immediately, "I was complimenting you. Can't you take a compliment?!"

"It doesn't matter, Mom. This time it is a compliment and other times it is criticism. Just stop it!"

"Okay, I won't say another word," she said in a childish voice as if she were so hurt she was going to take her toys and go home, stomping off from the playground.

This confrontation did not necessarily stop her, but I must admit that it is better—she does not venture into that territory much anymore. Given the reality that I cannot control my mother's response to my boundary, I, once again, am responsible for setting and enforcing limits with her. While I do care if I should hurt someone, my gauge for correct behavior is that my motive is pure (to care for myself), and I must stay with that.

❀ ❀ ❀

"That is what a daughter does."

Some boundaries I set were very firm, fixed and immutable, such as the one I set in the following circumstance. When my father was in in-home hospice, I spent three hours with him every Friday to give my mother a break. That continued until he was such a fall risk that I did not want the responsibility, since I was not trained to lift or help someone in that condition.

Yet, my parents would not hire an aide to come in. So, I set the boundary that I would not be alone with him nor be responsible for his safety and well-being.

I also added another limit, declaring that I would not bring him to the bathroom and care for those needs. My mother was not happy, telling me emphatically, "But he is your father! That is what a daughter does!"

What? Where did she come up with this?

Well, that is what my mother did for her father when he was dying. I respect her and applaud her for her caring help. But, this was not going to work for me—it felt sexual (not just squeamish) because of my father's previous covertly and emotionally incestuous behaviors. Whatever questions and thoughts I had, I kept to myself, just making sure she heard me.

❀ ❀ ❀

I *am* a Caretaker.

I take care; it is part of my nature. I am stating this as a positive because we usually place a negative connotation on the role of caretaker. And, I take this role seriously as daughter, mother, partner, and psychotherapist. In each of these capacities, I am susceptible to the negative aspects of caretaker. My profession, especially, can perfectly set me up to fall into its unhealthy side. I could not do the job I do without the boundaries I have set. Additionally, my 12-Step programs have given me phrases that I continue to rely on, such as, "There is a God and I am not it." "I am not responsible for other people's lives."

It is a challenge to draw that fine line between appropriate responsibility for my actions and falling into a co-dependent caretaker role. I am regularly tested as a therapist—especially when people are suffering and have much early wounding. In this profession, clients may make me their 'savior'. It is similar to the CEI dynamic in my family because it can creep up slowly and is hard to recognize until it is upon me. However, I continue to work on being aware and to have the patience, strength, and sensitivity to reflect the situation back to the client. My hope is to have them understand that the real healing comes from them and their work, with me as a collaborator.

Yet, sometimes I still get caught in the belief that I should have all the answers and that if the client does not get better, it is my fault. The truth is that I do not have all the answers and at times a client is not ready to make changes no matter how much they wish to. Occasionally I must refer a client to someone else because I have taken them as far as I can. As a therapist, and in all my relationships, I have come to recognize that qualities of sensitivity, honesty, support for growth, and knowing limits are essential.

Below, I'd like to encapsulate the lessons presented in this chapter.

BOUNDARIES

- A boundary is a border or limit that is permeable and flexible.
- You, yourself, are responsible for setting and enforcing a boundary. This includes

---

monitoring you own motives.

• The motive for a boundary MUST be self-care. Otherwise, it may be an attempt to threaten, control, get revenge, or manipulate the other person. If it is *anything other than self-care*, it will disrupt the relationship and cause more problems and pain.

• When beginning to set boundaries, you are at risk to be seen as the 'bad guy'. Tolerating this role is a must. Get support.

• Guilt may arise when you set a boundary. Guilt is a *withdrawal* symptom from surrogate-spouse, mediator, caretaker, and other co-dependent roles.

FORMULA FOR SETTING A BOUNDARY

• Tell the person how their behavior impacts you: "When you do this (specific behavior), I feel (emotions)." "When you say this (specific thing in this specific way), I feel (emotions)." E.g., "When you talk about Dad, I feel angry and sad."

• "If you continue to do, say (specific

behavior), I will (take an action), to take care of myself." E.g., "If you continue to talk about Dad, I will leave the room and return in an hour."

NOTE:

A feeling is **NOT**, "I feel like ..." or "I feel that..."

These are thoughts, not feelings. With these statements you are essentially saying, "I think that..."

With a feeling, you say, "I feel angry, sad, hurt, etc."

With a feeling you are essentially saying, "I am angry, sad, hurt, etc."

That is, you are directly expressing the emotions inside you.

THE GUIDE FOR SELF-CARE ACTIONS

Adapted from Imago Therapy, (Crapuchettes, 2005):

SMART

- Specific: "I am going to take a time-out and go into the other room."
- Measurable: "I am going into the other

room for an hour and check in with you afterward."

- **Attainable:** The other room is available. The action is possible and there is willingness to follow through.
- **Realistic:** Can I do this exactly as I say?
- **Timely:** The response is as close to the event as possible.

CONNECTING TO THE MOTHERSHIP

What does spirituality and a connection to the Divine (the MotherShip) have to do with Covert Emotional Incest? Everything. CEI is about feeling empty at your core. CEI robs you of being in touch with who you are and puts you into a role—the substitute spouse role—to take care of and focus on others. It objectifies you, stealing your humanity, reducing you to a role of 'thing' that is there for other people's pleasure. In these roles, there's a primal disconnect. Only a shell of yourself is left.

In order for anyone to establish a sense of connection and security we must have had the vital experience of attunement with a major caregiver(s). Attunement occurs when a parent is regularly responsive to their child's needs beginning in infancy. The infant/child learns that their parent (caregiver) is dependable, therefore their needs are met, and the world is a safe place.

When a parent, her-or-himself, hasn't gotten this as a child and has not done the psychotherapy work needed to feel full and whole, it becomes difficult to provide attunement to their own children. This is so, because on some level they are still children themselves; they may not have what is inherently necessary to parent effectively. In many cases, they cannot give what they haven't received, but, of course, there are exceptions to this. And, since a parent is a child's first example of an omnipotent being, this intrinsically translates to a relationship with the Divine (Kushner, 1995). The mis-attuned child will often lack the felt-sense of security and safety that a constant link to a loving Higher Power provides.

The "good enough mother" (Winnicott, 1953) or father, provides attunement imperfectly, yet consistently and timely. In my own story there was confusion, created by CEI, since I had the "good enough mother" (father) at times— even better than good enough. When my mother was there for me I felt seen, heard, loved, and safe— she could make everything okay, just as a connection with God can. Unfortunately, it was not predictable. So, I felt lost and insecure, searching for THAT mother and longing for connection with THAT mother. I didn't know when I was going to get her. I still don't. This type of conditioning is called intermittent reinforcement. It is the most potent form. Never knowing when the reward would drop, I kept going back, like a lab rat in behavioral psychology research pushing on the lever to get food. I don't fall into this trap nearly as often today because I am now aware it exists. I also monitor and adjust my expectations about it. However, I do see the craziness this dynamic caused and how the pattern generalized to my relationships with others. I became aware of its correlation to my feeling unsafe, and, even now, sometimes question whether the Divine, as the 'ultimate parent', is a steady force in my life.

Because of being stuck in the substitute spouse, related co-dependent and objectified 'thing' roles, I mistrusted my intuition. I looked to others to determine my truth. I now joke with my mother about her classic exclamation, "I am cold put a sweater on!" Now, we can say, "Oh that is just a Jewish mother." Well, maybe now, but as a kid, the implicit message was that I didn't know how I felt. I learned that my instincts were not accurate because my parents regularly defined my reality for me. Through their lens, they would dictate how I felt and what I needed.

The road to my current beliefs about, and link to, the Divine has been long and arduous. I have been a seeker all my life. My rabbi once told me that "holiness is in the seeking." Below are some stories of my trek to connection.

❀ ❀ ❀

Other than during religious rituals, my parents did not ask, answer, or facilitate discussion about God when I was growing up. This created a void in my heart and soul. As a little girl, I had felt so empty and wanted what my friends had—a regularly scheduled structure—going to church every Saturday evening. It seemed as though they had something I didn't, perhaps a contentedness, something that would fill the vacant hole I felt inside. I tried praying next to my bed at night as I saw on TV and as my friends told me about. It did nothing. I was going through the motions but that was about it and the feeling of desolation stayed with me. As my angst grew, I even went so far as to ask to go to church with my friends.

On the appointed day when I would join them, I was so excited and hopeful. I knew I would find at this church what was necessary to fill that hole. It didn't matter that I didn't know the 'worship' or whatever they did there. But, what I remember most was my friend instructing me not to tell anyone I was Jewish, otherwise lightning would strike, and I would be kicked out or killed. Clearly, this did not make for a sense of belonging or spiritual satisfaction (even though I would not have known those words), but I did as I was told. I was worried the whole time that someone would find out, and in my terrified imagination I could see the lightning coming through the roof and striking me dead. It might hit others too— blow the roof right off the place! *"Don't move, Adena, just sit still,"* I warned myself. So, I did. I sat quietly, and as a seven-year-old child, looked up at the bloody man nailed to a wooden cross with a wreath around his head, his face suffering in pain and defeat. I felt sad and afraid. *This is what I was supposed to pray to? This is what I was supposed to be filled by and saved by?* It just seemed weird and didn't fit at all. But there was still time, so at the end of the Mass, I shook people's hands and feigned being a Catholic, pretending I did this every week. That didn't work either and I was relieved to leave unscathed and unharmed. I knew I wasn't going back there again!

This wasn't for me; it was not my answer. However, it did not take away my envy and feeling of being left out every Saturday evening, as I watched my playmates and their families walk down the street. I now knew they were going somewhere I did not belong.

❀ ❀ ❀

Yet, there were moments that I knew I did belong to something greater than myself. These moments occurred when I was told stories of my people, the Jewish people. They were stories of our history. Stories of persecution, struggle and triumph (the Exodus, the Holocaust, and the establishment of the State of Israel). It was through these that I experienced a sense of oneness with generations of ancestors that brought meaning to my life.

Today, I am aware that beyond this collective history, a connection to Something Greater was elicited by certain rituals. One of these was our family's occasional trip to my paternal grandparents' apartment for Friday night Shabbat dinner. It was one of my favorite times as a kid. Praying with grandma over the candles—just like in the movie, *Fiddler on the Roof*—left me feeling a part of something significant. And all the special ethnic foods— chopped liver, chicken soup with homemade noodles, and, oh, the baking. I can still smell the latkes (potato pancakes). Their tantalizing aroma greeted us even before the fourth-floor elevator door opened.

Seder—my favorite holiday. Talk about ritual! My father, at the head of the table, directing, reading and telling the story of the Exodus. I loved when he told these stories. They made everything magical. It's one of the things I miss most about my father—his story telling— even though, as he got older, he told the same ones repeatedly. His tales were mostly about his childhood and how wonderful it was. Yes, the stories were repetitive, but I would pay anything to hear them all again from his lips.

❀ ❀ ❀

As I mentioned, God wasn't discussed in my home. Growing up I wondered, *"Is there really a God? How could there be if genocide like the Holocaust could happen? If so many terrible things happen to people?"* Sensitivity to suffering is a defining feature of my innate personality. As a three-year-old, my mom would read me the story *Are You My Mother?* (Eastman, 1960) about a little bird who lost its mother. I would cry because, on some unspoken level, I knew how that baby bird felt. I wept when I saw the movie, *Ryan's Daughter* (1970). I was particularly upset about Michael, John Mills' character, who was lame and the 'village idiot'. He was mocked and shunned; he didn't belong. Is this sensitivity to another's pain part of the makeup of anyone who is searching for a Higher Power or deeper meaning to life? A rhetorical question.

So, the longing continued and I persisted in my search.

❀ ❀ ❀

In high school, my friend Kenny was reading Ram Dass's book, *Be Here Now* (1971). I was fascinated and yearned to talk to Kenny about his seeking. Our friendship centered on drinking, so I don't think we took the time to talk when we were both sober. Therefore, I don't remember us speaking about it in a coherent manner, but do remember the strong desire for that conversation and for what I thought it would bring me. I always liked Kenny because I sensed a depth and soft spirit in him. Perhaps, when we know even one other person on the quest, it gratifies us. We were just too young for this type of conversation so, we only touched the tip of the iceberg as we sailed by in our teens.

Adolescence, itself, is a spiritual crisis. In *I'm Dancing as Fast as I Can,* a book by Barbara Gordon (1980), I related to the protagonist even though, at eighteen, I was much younger than she. I knew her pain, her craziness. Suicidality— the thoughts, the plans—resulted, for both of us, when there was no connection. A recurring nightmare from childhood that resurfaced was one in which I was unhinged, in a spacesuit with the hose not connected to the mothership. I was Frank in *2001 Space Odyssey* set adrift by Hal, the computer, searching to connect to Something!

Looking back on my spiritual quest, I see now that my addictive behaviors were some of the ways I attempted to achieve a spiritual experience. They were an attempt to fill the hole with anything outside myself. My addictions were my Higher Power, if you will. They drove my thinking, feeling and behaviors. I let them run me, gave them all my power. Alcohol was my God. It made me feel whole and accepted. Until it didn't. Until it created more pain, anguish, shame, humiliation, and loneliness than I had ever felt before. My best friend, lover, and Higher Power turned on me to become my biggest enemy, dragging me to places emotionally, physically and mentally that almost killed me.

How do I talk about my spirituality without talking about 12-Step programs? It was in those rooms where I retrieved my spirit and my soul was restored. I was taught that a 'spiritual awakening' was indeed a change in perception that would come as the result of following specific suggestions. This has absolutely been true for me and my perceptions continue to change, especially about God/the Divine. I saw miracles happening in myself and with others: Getting and staying sober; getting and remaining abstinent from all forms of compulsive eating; staying focused on me and my recovery instead of being scattered and blown about by outside forces. I consciously decided to use the 12-Step groups as my Higher Power.

This group force was invisible yet palpable. I experienced it in meetings with my eyes watering, my heart opening, and having surges of love and awe. These feelings were also affirmed by others in the group. This power provided what was necessary to work the program one day at a time, healing my eating disorder and alcoholism, and divesting of the caretaker, fixer and mediator roles. I believe the inner turmoil caused by CEI, tripped the trigger of my predisposition to many forms of the disease of addiction. Today, I see that unconditional love, along with practicing the spiritual principles of honesty, integrity, humility, willingness and acceptance are what gave me that power to overcome.

Female mentors or 'mothers of choice', both in and out of 12-Step programs, have been essential in developing and deepening my connection to the Divine. Being accepted and loved unconditionally by these women despite their awareness of my shameful behaviors and other faults, was key for me to continue evolving my concept of a Higher Power. If they could love me, so could God. My attachment to these women was another step in coming out of isolation and into connection. For me, the Divine often speaks through other people. "Let us love you until you can love yourself," was my mentors' message. They were my new role models for how to embody the Divine gracefully. They taught me, "Come from love and not fear." This has guided my heart, thoughts, and actions for quite some time. It has literally saved my life. I pause, ask, and answer, "What decision, action or thought is loving toward myself and others in this moment versus coming from fear?"

I am committed to have love be my driving force, yet aware and respectful of fear's role in human survival. Fear is the main feeling that stimulates our nervous system to take action, affording us a chance to stay alive. We would not have evolved without it. Growing up in the clutches of CEI created the fear of not being lovable, accepted and worthy; it felt like a life or death situation. Therefore, I unconsciously played the harmful roles of substitute spouse, caretaker, etc. that were laid out for me.

These women mentors also led me through a process in which they shared their experience, strength and hope, encouraging me to see my part in troubled relationships. Through them I learned to stop taking responsibility for others' choices, behaviors and feelings. I was never graded or judged, nor did I have to take care of these ladies in any way. What a relief! And corrective experience!

This proved what I was taught in my professional training, that "...trauma happens in relationship, so healing must happen in relationship." Not only does healing include nurturing relationships with others, it also embraces those with the Divine and the self. These relationships are both the essential healing elements for, and the results of, having worked through CEI.

As I've come to believe from my years of searching, our natural state is to be connected with the Divine. In this state we are relaxed and joyful. It is in fear and anxiety that we experience separation. My concept of God/the Divine/Higher Power has evolved over the years. Engaging in activities like singing at the top of my lungs (in the shower, karaoke, or driving) and belly- laughing from silly games played with friends goes a long way in keeping me connected. Walking along the beach, watching and listening to the crashing waves is another for-sure way to unite me with God.

Now, at fifty-five years of age, unconditional love is the energy I conceive to be my Higher Power. It is like an electric current— always there but not seen. Just as the current is always running, the energy from the Divine is always available. Being mindful of this availability has cured my terminal and frightening loneliness. I plug into the current and I am connected. I no longer fear being Frank, disconnected from the spaceship drifting off in isolation. I am seated comfortably and safely inside the MotherShip and I know it.

THE FACE OF FORGIVENESS

It didn't happen quickly, yet the recognition was profound. I was free, I was light, I was unburdened. Where did all the heaviness go? How did I get here? The 'here' I discovered is the internal state of forgiveness. This chapter is about the journey to this state as much as it is about the 'face' of forgiveness—what it looks and feels like.

The markers along the path of forgiveness became evident as I worked with my own healing journey as well as those of my clients. Some markers were small stones, easily brushed aside; some were boulders that had to be circumvented or moved with great effort and help from others. The journey is not complete (is it ever?) but is now in clearer focus. It's been long and winding, like a switchback trail up the steep sides of the Sierras. Certain segments were straight, some narrow, and some had side trails. I hope, as I name these markers, that others can find their place on the trail and feel affirmed that forgiveness is indeed a path and not a destination.

Do I have to forgive in order to heal? What does forgiveness really mean? These are questions I've asked myself and that have been asked of me. The answer to the first is a simple, but not simplistic "yes". Yes, I must forgive in order to be truly free of identification with the victim role. This identification keeps us bound to the perpetrator and trauma. Yes, because this bind keeps us in a loop of blame, shame, self-perpetration (addictive behaviors and self-abandonment), dishonesty with ourselves and others, and the unconscious seeking of destructive relationships. The complexities of the "yes" will be addressed later in this chapter. The answer to the second question about the meaning of forgiveness is also filled with qualifications, the main one being to sort out the definition of forgiveness.

To define a word or condition, a good first step is to say what it is NOT, just as a researcher posits a null hypothesis to rule out possibilities and come to his/her conclusion. So, that's where I'd like to start...

What forgiveness IS NOT:

- Condoning behavior that is unacceptable

and hurtful.

- Attempting to, or forgetting behavior and events that happened.
- Letting someone 'off the hook' for their behavior.
- Absolving the perpetrator of sin with no earthly consequences.
- Superficially deciding to forgive, and believing all is done. This actually bypasses the work that is required in the forgiveness process.

I had to make a search for my own definition of forgiveness, just as I did for the definition of a Higher Power. I explored concepts from different religions, philosophies and theories before I came to know for myself that forgiveness is *a process of letting go and understanding that is a gift to one's self.* It is a process and not an event. Additionally, forgiveness really has nothing to do with the other person. Because of the forgiveness journey, I have been freed from the bitterness, shame, guilt, hurt, and loneliness I had felt for such a long time. It has also freed me of the beliefs that had kept me attached to the those who hurt me and to the harmful situations that occurred. I could not bypass or skip over the process. "The only way out is through."

Do I need to forgive to heal or recover? Again, in my definition of forgiveness, yes. My definition being that forgiveness is a process of letting go and, understanding that, is a gift to one's self. Healing, grieving and forgiving, in my experience, are all of the same path, which consists of but is not limited to:

• Identifying, labeling and expressing feelings. Doing this in a safe way, in a safe place and with a guide, such as a mental health professional. (This means in a manner that does not hurt yourself or someone else.)

• Deciding somewhere in the process to let go and not get stuck and/or languish in the feelings when they come up, as they will naturally.

• Acknowledging these emotions, riding their wave, and letting them pass. Emotions last about thirty to ninety seconds and come in waves. It helps to remember that you can manage these feelings for thirty to ninety seconds.

• Identifying beliefs about yourself, others, the

world and God distorted by CEI. (God or whatever concept you choose.)

• Identifying and setting limits that are self-care directed, not meant for punishment or revenge. This includes if, how, and when you have contact with those who have harmed you.

• Practicing being gentle and kind to yourself and others.

• Creating a 'payoff and cost list' to identify what you get out of and what consequences you experience from the beliefs, feelings and behaviors that cause pain.

• Understanding yourself and what makes you tick—your motives, beliefs, behaviors, dreams, and feelings

• Understanding that CEI does not happen in a bubble; that it is most probably multigenerational and systemic, and knowing that you can begin to stop the cycle right now.

• Creating activities that get you out of the CEI dynamic and victim role. For example, formally 'resigning' from the surrogate spouse/confidant role.

• Sharing your experience, strength and hope with others who have also suffered from CEI.

In this process of forgiveness, I am also grieving losses such as my innocence as a young child and that CEI even happened at all. Grieving for the child whose life was 'cut short'; for the child who was lost in others' needs; for the child who will never have the mother or father she needed. I will not get a second chance at a childhood in which CEI does not exist. Continuing to seek this means the trauma is running my life. Being caught in this trap leads to behaviors that are not age-or developmentally-appropriate. If I were caught in the trap, my child and adolescent selves would be occupying my fifty-five-year-old body—driving my car, so to speak, and getting into the trouble children and adolescents get into. The grieving takes me to the place of acceptance of a lost childhood—it is over, and I can let go. I now have peace and meaningful adult relationships.

Another facet of the forgiveness, grieving and healing process was the acknowledgement of my role as survivor. I *did* survive my childhood and adolescence. I *am* here now as an adult. I had the opportunity to exchange the identity of victim for one of survivor. I had lived a long time with victim glasses on and saw the world through those distorted lenses. "Poor me" was my cry. I believed my parents and others needed to change, if I was to be happy. As I entered my mid-twenties, I began to see this prescription wasn't working. That was when I got new lenses and moved from the victim role to the survivor role, in which I did the bulk of my work to get a bridge built to the thriver role. This part of the journey takes the time it takes. It cannot be rushed. Patience and perseverance are necessary.

Today, I wear thriver glasses most of the time. When there is high stress however, I may find myself reaching for the survivor or even victim glasses. My recovery is evident in that it happens less often, and I grab for my thriver lenses more quickly.

Forgiving myself has been an important part of moving from victim to survivor and then to the thriver role. This, again, is the path of feeling and then letting go. I recognized and accepted that as a child I was purely a victim. I released myself from guilt and shame regarding decisions I made and behaviors I engaged in as a young person. These were outside of my values system and set me up to be in dangerous and humiliating situations. There are times when I still blame myself and get that 'shiver of shame'.

But now, because of moving through the forgiveness process, I have the freedom to choose what will affect me and how intensely I feel it. Currently an adult, I look back, hold myself accountable for my choices, and have great compassion for those younger selves. I have been able to do this through a combination of personal psychotherapy, 12-Step involvement, professional education, meaningful relationships, and soulful prayer and searching.

Client Responses

The above is my story of finding forgiveness, so here I would like to share some concerns, questions, and recognitions from clients I have worked with.

- Clients generally struggle with the 'nots' of forgiveness and the importance of recognizing them. But when they finally understand them, it affords great freedom.
- They like the concept of progression from victim to survivor to thriver.
- Sometimes clients do not want to forgive

sometimes, but when they see that they have choices, limits, and boundaries that titrate the experience, they like being responsible for their own needs and levels of forgiveness.

• Once they have 'resigned' from the roles put upon them by others, clients learn they can redefine and embody these roles in a new way. For example, the caretaker role can be transformed into caregiving. The client thereby cares for him or herself while helping others in a healthy manner. In doing so, the client retains a beautiful and valuable part of themselves.

• Clients often struggle with spiritual and religious issues regarding forgiveness. Examples of this include expressing anger at God for allowing abuse to happen to them and others, and for God not answering prayers to have the abuse stop.

• Clients also have questions such as: Does God forgive me? Do I have to forgive God? Does God forgive the perpetrator? When these issues and questions arise, it is essential to explore a client's religious and spiritual beliefs in conjunction with the forgiveness process.

Finally, I share with clients that I, myself, continue to accept forgiveness as a process. That there are times when I am in the flow and feel the freedom and peace that it brings. And, there are times when I get blocked again and need to go back to the practices listed above. I share the gratitude to have concrete steps and actions that return me to this flow and freedom. It's the 'rotor-rootering' of my yuck and muck- filled plumbing! Because it cannot be stated enough, I again say, "The forgiveness process is the grieving process is the healing process. It never ends, and it continues to elate and challenge."

Bumps and Switchbacks on the Road

What does forgiveness look like with my mother? After a lifetime of having her over identify with me, all I wanted was to be separate, to be my own self. Yet, when I gave birth to my son I was so frightened. I saw myself needing my mother in a way I had not imagined. I was trembling holding this little life. So, I called my mother an hour after Ian was born. She and my father were there within minutes. My body calmed and 'frightened' turned to 'excited' when I saw them both. Especially my mother. I was so happy to share this moment with her. There I was, the child feeling that everything would be okay now, *Mom* was here. She knew exactly how to hold my baby, how to soothe him. She had the patience of a saint. I trusted that she would be there for me, as a good and appropriate mother. I also knew she would be there for my son. All this proved to be true.

In the first few weeks of Ian's life, the responsibility of being a new mother weighed in at my core. I had many feelings, from great hope to terror, insecurity, and even anger about my basic needs being sacrificed. The conflict between "What about me?" and "I would give my life for this being" presented itself. My focus shifted from what I needed and wanted to pure love and commitment to this child. It was at this time, at thirty-two years of age, that I saw my mother in a different light. She wasn't the mom and I, the child. She now was more than my mother with and against whom I had struggled. She was a human being who took on the roles of caring mother and grandmother—the ones she believed she had been created for. I had new- found respect and empathy for all the feelings and needs that she had to juggle as a mother. I saw her mother-to-mother and woman-to- woman.

Was this the beginning of forgiveness? Perhaps, but another milestone in forgiveness with my mother and father occurred during a therapy session when I was thirty-six and struggling again with boundaries.

"Should I ask my parents to come in for family therapy?" I questioned.

The look on my therapist's face told me everything.

"It isn't about my parents any more, is it?" I asked rhetorically.

"No, it is about you now. You are an adult. Your life is your responsibility," she responded, almost unnecessarily.

Accepting my responsibility, and accepting my parents who they were, faults and all, was also a demonstration of forgiveness. I could no longer blame them or expect them to be different. The focus had to be on me and how I was going to change *my* reactions and work out *my* difficulties. My sanity and happiness could not depend on my parents doing it differently any longer. I was willing to let go of the relationship if necessary. There was a lightness that came upon me. I had been playing tug of war with them since my adolescence and I finally let go of the rope. I was free of the CEI dynamic in a way I had never been before. I was powerless over my parents' behavior, but not over what was going on inside me. I never wanted to pick up that rope again.

I believe this next story of my mother and me, shows a level of forgiveness I never dreamed possible—it is a major switchback that I took to get me up the side of that mountain.

Mom broke her shoulder and I chose to be her caregiver. This was an intentional and adult choice, not an obligation of the child caretaker. Of course, bathing her was part of the deal and I was hesitant because it meant I would be getting undressed as well and she would see my naked body. Talk about exposed! This was just the scenario that might bring objectifying comments as had happened so often in the past. Constant comments about my body, my build, my weight, etc. I did not want to leave myself open to that possibility, but I did want to help. I weighed out what I wanted and needed more— to help, be vulnerable, or to 'protect' myself. I decided it was worth the risk of being vulnerable and having my boundaries violated. So, I made the conscious choice to get in the shower with her. As we were standing in the shower together, I realized I did not feel threatened or compromised. No comment was made about my body. It was a miracle! As I was washing her hair we began to laugh. We laughed so hard that tears were running down our faces. Tears of relief and joy about how the long-term tension between us was gone. What was left was just love, a pure mother-daughter love. My appreciation abounds.

Another major scramble on the road of forgiveness appeared at the end of my father's life. I came upon a giant boulder—the one I had turned away from in fear for many years. That fear was of losing him. But, then I saw that events and my own growth were creating a path around it. Yes, I didn't want him to die, but I accepted his death was inevitable. I wanted to be there for both of my parents while maintaining healthy boundaries. This was a challenge due to old patterns of manipulation and rescuing. The inpatient hospice experience had been extremely difficult for my father. He was delirious at night and so frightened to die. I believe he knew he would not return home when he checked into the hospice residence. I was able to remain steadfast; to be emotionally and physically available to both my parents during this painful and challenging time, while maintaining my boundaries.

Below, I share the notes I wrote about my father's death because I believe it is a snapshot of what forgiveness looks like and feels like.

❀ ❀ ❀

March 8, 2015, 6 AM

I hear the death rattle. Scott and I quickly get to the bedside, holding Dad's hands and telling him we love him. I dial Mom's number and just as she answers he takes his last breath. Mom screams and cries, "He's dead! He died!" I was breathing slowly and deeply. My body was calm throughout. Settled. Grateful. Moved. An awe-inspiring spiritual experience just as I had heard so many others had when their loved ones passed. This is the type of experience I had wanted so badly, but I had been warned by my sponsor to watch my expectations. Maybe I would not be there when he died.

Turning back to the bed, I looked up to my right and said, "I love you, Dad. I am so glad you are okay." I felt him there. I knew he was there and not in his body any longer. Actually, he mostly left it the day prior. It was obvious. I told Scott, but he didn't believe me. Not that I had expected him to—Scott does not believe in any of this stuff. Neither does Mom. However, this whole experience, the knowing, gives me solace because I feel it in my bones that it is real and true. I did everything I needed to and said everything I needed to while he was here on earth. What I also feel in my bones is that my path with Dad has been taken to a higher level.

❀ ❀ ❀

These vignettes demonstrate the importance of the personal work necessary for clarity about the following:

• Knowing the difference between caring and care-taking, thereby maintaining firm boundaries with my mother.

• Seeing my parents as human with both shortcomings and strengths.

- Understanding that due to unexamined issues, my parents unknowingly foisted the abuse of CEI upon me.

- Recognizing that I, now an adult, am responsible for my own life. Expecting my parents to change is unrealistic and keeps me stuck in old patterns.

- Making a conscious decision about what risks to take, with whom and when.

- Healing enough so that I was totally present with my father in his last hours. No hiding pain, no false bravado. Just real feelings of loss and sadness for a man whom I called Dad and who was such a bright star in my constellation.

These markers and this path could never have been plotted or fabricated. The journey could never have been rehearsed. For all moments and for the health I have achieved to have been able to experience them fully, I am truly grateful.

THE NEXT GENERATION

Perfectionism played a significant role in my mothering. This is expected, given my history with CEI. I pressured myself to do everything 'right' so I would not totally mess up my son. I was determined to do all the things I thought my mother and father did right and none of the things they did wrong. I had read about Winnicott's (1953) "good enough mother" theory, which was helpful. From it I ascertained that I did not have to be perfect and meet Ian's every need every minute of every day. I just had to do it well enough. But, what does that mean? Being a professional psychotherapist, I studied a lot about attachment theory and "good enough" parenting so I had some knowledge and skills my own parents were not afforded. I also had my 12-Step recovery, which taught and reinforced the following concepts: boundaries, allowing someone to be who they are, and the pitfalls of co-dependency. Yet, for all my studies, I needed and sought help and feedback from other mothers—

those who had walked before me.

A couple of years prior to conceiving, while sitting on my friend's back patio having tea one afternoon, I asked, "As a mother and wise woman, what is your best advice for me about being a mother myself?" "Let me read you something," she said gently. She got up from her chair, went into the house and when she returned I listened to this—an excerpt from Khalil Gibran's *The Prophet* (1923, p.17):

> And a woman who held a babe against
> her bosom said, "Speak to us of
> Children."
> And he said:
>> Your children are not your children.
>> They are the sons and daughters of
>> Life's longing for itself.
>> They come through you
>> but not from you.
>> And though they are yours, they
>> belong not to you.
>> You may give them your love but
>> not your thoughts.
>> For they have their own thoughts.
>> You may house their bodies but

not their souls,

For their souls dwell in the house

of tomorrow, which you cannot

visit, not even in your dreams.

You may strive to be like them,

but seek not to make them like

you.

For life goes not backward nor

tarries with yesterday.

You are the bows from which

your children

as living arrows are sent forth.

The archer sees the mark upon

the path of the infinite, and

He bends you with His might that

His arrows may go swift and far.

Let your bending in the archer's

hand be for gladness;

For even as he loves the arrow

that flies, so He loves also the

bow that is stable.

My mouth hung open. My heart was overflowing with joy and relief, as if I had just heard the words of God. I was profoundly affected and knew intuitively this philosophy was a compass I would follow in raising my son, Ian.

The idea that I was being entrusted with my baby's life but he or she would never be 'mine' reconfigured my entire notion of parenthood. This notion was definitely not what my parents conferred to me. The whole concept touched a very sensitive chord because I had felt 'owned' by my parents. Part of that brought security—I knew where I belonged and knew I was loved—but being 'owned' also had what felt like a smothering or choking grip on me. I had to break away from the nest rather than fly away naturally. I was committed to ensure that my child's wings would be strong and the nest supportive enough so he could fly when the time was right.

In addition to Winnicott and Gibran, the forming of my mother role was influenced by Harville Hendrix and Helen Hunt's Imago Relationship Therapy model, which I began studying in the early nineties. They propose that a healthy parent "gives the love that heals" (1998). Validation and empathy are key components of this type of love. It was my hope that utilizing these would lead to Ian feeling 'seen' and accepted for who he was. Being mirrored in this way is part of what creates secure attachment, meaning safe connection with me and feeling the stability of my love and support when he ventures out.

Part of nurturing Ian's secure attachment was the commitment to have him grow up in a recovery household: I was sober, abstinent from eating disorder behaviors, and continuing in psychotherapy and 12-Step programs. And, as for the topic of this book, CEI, it was clear that I should not rely on my child for emotional support and that he would not be responsible for my emotional needs. As expected, there were times when I went to the other extreme, declaring that I would NEVER rely on Ian in any way.

This absolute way of thinking has always gotten me into trouble. It is simplistic, not realistic. It led me to put unattainable expectations on myself and the relationship with my son, cementing the shaming belief that I am a failure. And so, over the years, I sensed something was askew, but only in this last year did I recognize and name it. The 'it' was the fact that my fear of perpetrating the same hurts and expectations on Ian as my parents did on me, kept me in certain ways from acting naturally with him. I would think this happens when anyone acts under a rigid set of rules and regulations—the natural flow is inhibited. This rigidity and fear kept me, at times and in certain circumstances, from being real with my son.

So, armored (was I going into battle?) and carrying all this information, how was I to keep my footing, my balance? How was I to have boundaries, validate, empathize, etc., and still be a regular mom?

This continues to play out even now that Ian is in his twenties. For example, is it acceptable for me, the parent, to have needs in the relationship with my young adult child? If so, what constitutes appropriate? CEI taught me to believe I was not to have needs of my own, but was here to meet the needs of others. This was reinforced by romantic partners when I would finally ask for something I was told that I was needy and/or dramatic. Or, my request was dismissed. If my needs were met, I would have a hard time receiving because of the primary belief of not deserving. This dilemma is painful. Given my history with CEI, it is also predictable.

A short time ago, I noticed I was disturbed about a pattern of interaction with Ian and not sure how to handle it. My first reaction was to invalidate and deny my need, telling myself, *"You are the adult and he is the child. If you let him know you want something from him, you are perpetrating the CEI dynamic and laying a burden upon him."* I was terribly conflicted. I spoke with my wife, my support system, and then finally my therapist.

My therapist questioned, "Is it never okay for you to have a need in your relationship with your son?"

"No, isn't that putting my stuff on him? I do not want to do to him what was done to me. I have been committed to that from day one. Really, even before day one."

"Well, as he is coming into adulthood, I would challenge that your need or desire for reciprocity in your relationship with your son is not perpetrating the CEI dynamic. The belief you have about it not being acceptable to have needs is pervasive in your life when it comes to relationships. What has it cost you?"

This all was a big stretch for me. I had to investigate and remain curious about my rigidity regarding this prohibition. I also had to confront my assumption that it was automatically CEI.

"What about *how* you express your need?" asked my therapist.

"Help me, I have no idea." I replied. "Maybe something like this, 'Ian, I would like to be able to talk to you about what I am doing and have you get to know me more, now that you are an adult. Are you willing to do that?'"

"You know, it is amazing, because if this were with anyone else, I would have no problem saying something like that. I would also suggest the exact thing to a client. Asking for reciprocity. I can do that. I have done that. My rule about the definition of the mother role and the son role is getting in the way here. Is it really reasonable that I ask this of him?"

"Yes, and it is probably very important for his growth. It is another way for him to see how his behavior impacts someone he cares about and you are giving him an opportunity to mature."

I mulled this over for another month or so trying to find the right time to say this or something like it. As happens with most matters, the opportunity presented itself spontaneously during a phone conversation we were having about something else. The perfect words just flowed out of my mouth.

In response, Ian laughed and then said, "I had no idea you wanted this Mom. Yeah, I am happy to do that. I am sorry if you felt bad."

"Aha! There is the son I know and love!" I took a deep breath and thanked the universe for supplying the words and providing the ideal timing. I could not have planned this. I also heard a voice say, *"It is okay for you to have this need or desire. It is really okay."* Another big sigh and a sense of serenity.

Gratitude came over me for this encounter and how I was moving out of my fear and fixed ideas about parenting. Feeling connected with my son in this way is a gift I receive from my continued willingness to grow, change, and confront my history of CEI. Even in our new-found reciprocity, I remain conscientious of what details I share with Ian about my past and the CEI dynamic. I have allowed him to have a relationship with his grandparents unburdened by my particular history with them. I have learned what 'appropriate needs' mean in regard to my adult son. I now know that it is natural to have these needs and beneficial to state directly what they are.

❀ ❀ ❀

"It's My Body!"

Having a CEI and physical sexual abuse history, I was trained to believe my body was not my own. I believed it was for others to comment on, touch, grab, hug too tight or for too long. I had no choice. And again, I was determined to not allow this to happen to my child. Reading a book titled *It's My Body* (Britain, 1982) to Ian in early childhood was empowering to him and I have to say, to me as well—the young parts of me, especially.

"No, It's my body!" I heard Ian say sternly one morning when he was a year and a half. I went into my parents' kitchen to find him with his hands on his hips and my parents with stunned yet amused looks on their faces.

"We went to pick him up and hug him and this is what we got!" they exclaimed while chuckling a bit. "What have you been teaching him?"

"I have been teaching him that he gets to say who, when and how others touch him. It is HIS body and he gets to choose." I found I was declaring this for myself as much as for my son.

That day, we all read the book together sitting on the living room couch. I will never forget all of us saying out loud together, in support of Ian's autonomy, "No touch. It's my body!"

❀ ❀ ❀

Like Mother, Like Son?

When Ian was in fourth grade, my resolve to be a good mother and to allow her son his life as it would be presented to him, was tested. The year was all set: The perfect teacher—the teacher *I* had wanted for Ian, the one *I* knew would be good for him. And then I got the letter.

"Mrs. Lees, we regret to inform you that Ms. Jones will be on leave and not teaching fourth grade this coming year. A new teacher has been hired and will take over the class. This new teacher has many years' experience, so we are confident your son will receive the level of excellence our school provides."

What – how could they?!?!? My body began to tremble and tears rolled down my face. "No!" I yelled out loud. *"What is going to happen to him? He has to have the teacher I knew he would do well with!"* My next thought was, *"What do I need to do to assure Ian gets into another class, with the next-best teacher?"* I immediately called a friend whose son had finished fourth grade the previous year and loved his teacher. I was given the name, hung up the phone and then called the school. "I need to get my son into Ms. Smith's class next year, I said, rather frantically, to the administrative assistant. "I am not able to help you with this, Mrs. Lees. Would you like to speak with the principal?" "Yes! Please!" I exclaimed.

I could not keep my cool. My voice was

quivering, loud and pressured. I was lucky enough to get the principal on the phone right away. I had been volunteering in my son's classes since kindergarten and was very involved, so the principle and I had a good relationship.

"Adena, I first want to assure you that Mrs. Brady, our new teacher is fabulous. I know her from another school and Ian will be well taken care of."

"I don't care, John," I said, "I do not know her and Mrs. Smith came highly recommended. I want to have Ian in her class. How can we make that happen?"

"I am afraid we can't. Mrs. Smith's class if full."

Thwarted, I started to panic. My breath became shallow, my heart beating out of my chest, my forehead sweaty and my mouth dry.

"So, I have to accept this?"

"Yes. I again assure you that Mrs. Brady is very qualified and Ian will get all that he needs next year."

I sunk into resignation. I wasn't going to pull Ian out of that school. I loved that school and knew he was thriving there. *"And acceptance is the answer to all my problems today..."* rang in my head. It is a writing from the Alcoholics Anonymous "Big Book" (2001) that had saved my behind many times.

My wife was in the room to witness this whole dramatic performance. "Adena, you need to calm down. You are totally overreacting."

"No, I am not! What is going to happen to Ian?" Out the window flew 'the acceptance'.

"I really think you need to check in and see where this reactivity is coming from. It is much bigger than the situation warrants. You know that when this happens there is something from your life that triggers this level of fear." Calming, reasonable and correct words from Diane.

"Yes, you are right. Ok, I will do my best." And then I really started to cry. Sob, actually. Diane came over and held me.

"Fourth grade was so terrible for me. I was bullied so badly and felt so powerless and helpless to do anything about it," came out of my mouth through the sobs. The feelings overwhelmed me, the grief, pain and fear. It was as if that scene from so many years ago was happening right then in that moment. I was nine-years-old in Diane's arms, sobbing about how painful it was to be me in this no-win situation. The teacher didn't notice, or if he did, he didn't do anything. My father gave me all kinds of psychological interventions and explanations for the bullying. My mother listened intently to my stories, but no adult stepped in for me. I couldn't fix or stop it on my own.

So, this was what my panic was about. To have the 'right' teacher meant the adult would be present who would protect my son/protect me. But now, it was critical that I separate my reaction and history from Ian and his experience. This was how I could parent effectively and not put my feelings and trauma on him.

I must say that after I cried in Diane's arms and had this "aha", my body settled and I was back in my adult parent-self. I had perspective and chose to trust the principal's recommendation. This recognition happened quickly, I believe, because I had done this type of work many times before. I was warned early on that when my son hit the developmental stages I had difficulty with as a child, these difficulties and their related feelings would surface. Here it was again.

Fast forward, Mrs. Brady turned out to be Ian's favorite teacher in all his years in elementary school! So much for *my* plans!

❀ ❀ ❀

Present-Day Parent

At this time, Ian is twenty-three and I see myself in the consultant role, not hands-on parent. I am there for him when he asks and needs guidance and will tell him if I see he is in danger of any sort. I am able now to ask him without fear or self-recrimination, "Would you like me to just listen or do you want feedback?"

As I have reported before, I was absolutely determined to not replicate the CEI dynamic with my child. Being in the mental health field was a great plus for me because I was exposed to and had access to information about attachment: How the mother-child bond impacts child development; what a healthy mother-child relationship is that creates security and autonomy. What is clearer than ever for me is that it is not permissible for a parent to put their *emotional* needs on that child. The parent is there to meet the child's needs, not the other way around. It is never okay to put children in the middle of the parents' relationship.

However, in a healthy relationship between a parent and a young-adult or adult-child, I do believe it is reasonable to ask for certain needs. For example, reciprocity in sharing our knowledge, in sharing our likes and dislikes, and in sharing our feelings when appropriate. And, yes, there is a role-reversal when parents get old and sick. The relationship can and does change to a point.

I continue to discover more as my son and I move through different developmental phases. As a result, our relationship is in an ongoing process of positive change. There are struggles and psychic pain, along with joy and celebration. This then, is what it has meant for me to be in a *Healing Process*, rather than to be healed or cured.

So, yes, you can be a survivor of CEI, have children and do healthy parenting. You are not doomed to repeat what happened to you. You will get triggered when your child reaches the stages of development or ages you were when you struggled. Especially at these junctures, it is critical to get help for yourself so you can separate your own issues from hers/his.

In addition to Ian entering fourth grade, this has occurred for me at different times throughout his childhood and adolescence. My own fear and self-centeredness get in the way sometimes in thinking he will feel and respond as I do and have done. Yet, he is a different person with different needs, viewpoints and responses. I just need to be reminded—and, thank God, Ian does remind me.

PULLING IT ALL TOGETHER

In this last chapter, the main aspects of CEI are presented. The format employed will, hopefully, help give a clear idea of the causes, the symptom-picture, and the steps to healing for those who have been affected by CEI. Using the framework below as a checklist for yourself will help you gauge your own journey as you repair the past and restore a healthful life that is your due.

CEI is a form of sexual abuse that can be highly confusing due to its often-subtle nature. It does not appear to be sexual because there may not be genital contact, however, as discussed previously, there is a high degree of sexual energy present. Additionally, this dynamic may be unconscious and/or not acknowledged by any of those involved.

Certain behaviors and relational interactions may appear as co-dependent, but the obfuscation of parental-child boundaries is more devastating in CEI because of the underlying spousal-sexual role component. Persons who have experienced CEI will often find themselves exhibiting behaviors similar to those who have a history of physical sexual abuse and, therefore, may spend much time and energy trying to find a memory of such abuse. This final statement is not to discourage that search but to suggest that the path to healing of CEI be undertaken simultaneously when appropriate.

Each of the following sections is on its own page and I suggest that you approach them as a workbook—check-marking the phrase, writing in the margins, highlighting, and coming back to it periodically.

Finally, I wish you only the best on your restorative journey.

Components of CEI

1. Lack of and/or violation of boundaries:
   a. Inconsistent adherence to intergenerational boundary.
   b. Triangulation.
   c. Distorted definition of emotional closeness.
   d. Enmeshed relationship with caregiver/parent(s).

2. Presence of 'creepy factor': e.g., touch, hugs too tight, kisses on the lips, sexual jokes or comments.

3. Substitute/surrogate spouse role. The child is
   a. Made confidant to one or both parents.
   b. Used as 'emotional mistress/master'.
   c. Expected to fix family members' personal and marital problems (fixer or mediator role).
   d. Required to meet parents' unmet needs (caretaker role).
   e. Emotionally-seduced to remain in co-dependent roles by being made to feel special and indispensable.

4. Pseudo-maturity is produced and reinforced.

5. Child is expected to be inappropriately loyal, for example, by being implicitly or explicitly directed to keep secrets from the other parent.

6. Autonomy is discouraged:
   a. Social life is diminished.
   b. Unacceptable to be your own person, with own needs or thoughts.

7. Sexual Objectification of child:
   a. Parent(s) keen and improper focus on child's body.
   b. Child sees self as commodity to be used by others.
   c. Exposed to age inappropriate and/or overwhelming sexual information.
   d. May produce premature sexual activity.

NOTES:

AFTEREFFECTS OF CEI

1. Unhealthy intimate relationships:
    a. Chooses unhealthy partners.
    b. Struggles to say "No" and set limits with others.
    c. Overly focused on meeting others' needs.
    d. Can be sexually promiscuous.
    e. Denies and avoids sexual and/or romantic interactions.
    f. Has emotional and/or physical affairs.
    g. Fears being open and vulnerable with others.
    h. Reenacts painful relationships.
    i. Feels torn between spouse and parent(s).
    j. Experiences self as 'having an affair' with mother or father.
    k. Others confront you for 'having an affair' with mother or father.

2. Poor sense of self:
    a. Distrusts own perceptions and hunches.
    b. Alternates between feeling special and inadequate.
    c. Blames self for others' mistreatment of

them.

    d. Has unrealistic standards and expectations of self (perfectionism).

    e. Is unaware of own likes, dislikes, and needs.

    f. Has exaggerated sense of feeling special when meeting parent'(s') emotional needs.

    g. Has a distorted sense of power over parent'(s') and others' lives.

    h. Believes "I do not have a right to need anything."

    i. Believes "Who I am and what I do is never enough."

    j. Feels overly responsible for others' wellbeing.

    k. Roles define self (surrogate spouse, caretaker, mediator, fixer, etc.).

3. Sexual difficulties:

    a. Feels like a sexual possession.

    b. Has a pattern of being mistreated sexually.

    c. Is overly focused on meeting others' sexual needs.

    d. Denies own sexual needs and/or desires.

    e. Compulsively uses pornography and/or

other sexual behaviors.

    f. Has sexual fantasies targeted to confirm self-worth.

    g. Pleases others sexually to feel good about her/himself.

    h. Derives an excessive sense of power when pleasing others sexually.

    i. Dissociates (e.g., not feeling present in body, emotional numbing) during sex.

4. Faulty boundaries:

    a. Struggles to say "No" and set limits with others.

    b. Interferes and attempts to manage others' conflicts.

    c. Experiences exaggerated guilt when practicing self-care.

    d. Has difficulty recognizing when being used and/or abused.

5. Mental health and compulsive behaviors:

    a. Has depression, suicidal thoughts, and/or anxiety.

    b. Struggles with post traumatic stress symptoms, ranging from high anxiety to emotional numbing.

    c. Exhibits pattern of dissociation as response to stress.

    d. Overuses alcohol, prescription and street drugs.

    e. Over/under-eats.

    f. Engages in pattern of purging (vomiting, laxatives, exercise).

    g. Compulsively spends/debts, and/or works.

6. Spiritual Struggles:

    a. Experiences a significant sense of emptiness and separateness from others and 'all that is'.

    b. Feels anger and conflict with or about God or a Higher Power.

NOTES**:**

SUGGESTIONS FOR HEALING (not necessarily in progressive order):

- Acknowledge there is a problem.
- Name it: get a context for what has or is happening in your family of origin.
- Get professional help from someone who knows about CEI.
- Talk about what has or is happening to you in a safe environment.
- Develop a healthy support system.
- Get accurate information and education about CEI and related issues (see references).
- Identify, label and express your feelings in a constructive way.
- Recognize you were a victim and now a survivor.
- Determine personal strengths and nurture them.
- Learn to trust your intuition.
- Acknowledge and appreciate yourself for the brilliance of adapting coping strategies to survive (survival skills).
- Identify which survival skills may not be working any longer.

- Focus on yourself and your needs first, not forgetting about others.
- Set and enforce boundaries.
- Give yourself permission to be human and make mistakes.
- Grieve all losses (childhood, ideal parents, etc.).
- Participate in 12-Step or other self-help programs when and where appropriate.
- Practice a daily routine of quiet reflection and gratitude.
- Develop a sense of humor about family dysfunction.
- Forgive self and others (see The Face of Forgiveness chapter).
- Find something you are passionate about and do it.
- Develop a relationship with 'something greater' than yourself that brings peace.
- Be willing to change or end relationships that perpetuate the CEI pattern and after-effects.
- Be the parent to yourself that you wished you would have had.
- Have fun!

NOTES:

WHAT IS IMPORTANT TO ADDRESS IN PSYCHOTHERAPY (not necessarily in this order):

- CEI family dynamics.
- How the nervous system is impacted by CEI and what this means for healing.
- Development of constructive ways to self-soothe and regulate your nervous system.
- Methods to stay present in your body, being able to think and feel at the same time.
- The benefits and rationale for psychiatric evaluation.
- Identifying precipitators to negative thoughts, feelings and behaviors.
- Identifying, labeling, and expressing emotions.
- The use of mood altering substances and/or behaviors.
- Healthy eating, nutrition, and exercise.
- Historical development of maladaptive coping strategies.
- Getting stuck in a destructive role (victim, surrogate spouse, caretaker, etc.).
- Sexual difficulties.
- Marital/couple conflict.
- Setting and maintaining healthy boundaries.

- Trusting and following intuition.
- Benefits of social support.
- Transformation of perfectionism and other distorted beliefs associated with CEI.
- Processing of old wounds to remove emotional charge.
- Grief issues—loss of childhood and ideal parent(s).
- Directly resolving issues with family members to include family therapy sessions when appropriate.
- Changing current behaviors that perpetuate the abuse and victim identity.
- Forgiveness of self and others.
- Spiritual questions and concerns.
- Balancing work and play.
- Making meaning of your experience.
- Celebrating who you are and who you are becoming.
- The importance of continuing to ask for help.

NOTES:

Victim ... Survivor ... Thriver

Below is a concise chart by Barbara Whitfield (2011) that I have found very helpful for myself and my clients. In it she addresses three roles or modes of thinking and acting as a result of trauma. These roles are the lenses through which to view yourself and the world. This chart is also a good diagnostic tool to see how you are doing.

Through time, and with the help of healing modalities, the 'victim' becomes a 'survivor' who begins to shed the trauma identity and has an intonation of strength. Eventually, he or she develops into a 'thriver' in which the trauma identity is much reduced. During times of crisis and stress, one can fall back into the earlier two roles, but may find him or herself out of them much more quickly.

VICTIM	SURVIVOR	THRIVER
"Depression"	Movement of feelings	Aliveness
Doesn't deserve to enjoy life	Struggling to heal	Gratitude for everything in life
Low self-esteem / shame / unworthy	Sees self as wounded and healing	Sees self as an overflowing miracle
Hyper-vigilant	Learning to relax	Able to experience peace
Confusion and numbness	Learning to grieve, grieving past ungrieved trauma	Grieving at current losses
Hopeless	Hopeful	Faith in self and life
Hides personal story	Not afraid to tell their story to safe people	Transforms to hero's journey
Feels defective	Compassion for others and eventually self	Open heart for self and others
Often wounded by unsafe others	Learning to protect self by "share-check-share"	Protects self from unsafe others
Places own needs last	Learning healthy needs	Places self first
Creates one drama after another	Sees patterns	Creates peace
Believes suffering is the human condition	Feeling some relief	Finds joy and peace
Serious all the time	Beginning to laugh	Seeing humor in life
Inappropriate humor, teasing	Feels associated painful feelings	Uses healthy humor
Numb or angry around toxic people	Increased awareness of pain and dynamics	Healthy boundaries with all people
Lives in the past	Aware of patterns	Lives in the Now
Angry at religion	Understanding the difference between religion / spirituality	Enjoys personal relationship with a Higher Power

ACKNOWLEDGEMENTS

This last page is almost as difficult to write as any because its scope is immense—how can I thank all who have been part of this expedition, helping in one way or another? I cannot, so I will just say that a giant 'thank you' is in order for several wise and committed persons I have encountered along my recovery journey.

First and foremost, to my editor, Francesca Toscani. There are no words to describe the creative influence your guidance and encouragement have had on me. You helped produce an author, a real author. I am ever so grateful for your wisdom, sense of humor, and expertise as a wordsmith. I could not have done this without you. Along with this, is appreciation to Dr. Kate Hudgins, who introduced us—you were right, Kate.

Thank you, Sally Rogers Devine, my intuitive and gifted graphic artist. You always know what images are in my heart and make them a reality. The cover you created for this book projects my intention and message perfectly—and it is beautifully done.

In humility and gratitude to all my 12-Step sponsors. You have shown me that healing and recovery are possible. Through your example I have learned to live a sober life of integrity and grace. Thank you for confronting and holding me accountable for my BS.

To Mary Kiernan-Tighe, my spiritual sister, an eternal thank you for your consistent and strong conviction that my story be told and this book be completed. Hashing things out with you, sobbing, and then laughing hysterically were all pieces I could do with only you.

Wendy Maltz, I appreciate your time and expertise in exploring the most authentic and effective way to get my message of covert emotional incest and its healing process out to the public.

Of course, I cannot omit all the clients and trainees I have had the privilege of guiding and collaborating with over the years. You have all taught me more than you could ever imagine.

Lastly, great thanks to Diane B. Schiff, my best friend, wife and informal editor. Your belief in me and of this book's message kept me moving forward when I so wanted to give up and go back to what is safe and familiar. Without your keen sense of literary clarity and simplicity, I would have gotten lost in the details and overwhelming feelings of the stories shared in these pages.

References, Sources, Bibliography

Adams, K. (2011, 1991). *Silently seduced: When parents make children their partners.* Deerfield Beach, FL: Health Communications Inc.

Bass, E., & Davis, L. (1988). *Courage to heal.* New York: HarperCollins Publishers. 1st Edition.

Britain, L. (1982). *It's my body: A book to teach young children how to resist uncomfortable touch.* Seattle, WA: Parenting Press.

Buber, M. (2010, 1923). *I and thou.* Eastford, CT: Martino Publishing.

Definition of Objectification. Retrieved from: http://dictionary.cambridge.org/us/dictionary/english/objectification

Definition of Reenactment.: Retrieved from: http://www.bernsteininstitute.com/traumatic-reenactment/

Definition of Sexual Objectification: Retrieved from: https://en.wikipedia.org/wiki/Sexual_objectification

Carnes, P. (1997). *The betrayal bond: Breaking free of exploitive relationships.* Deerfield Beach, FL: Health Communications, Inc.

Crapuchettes, B. (2005). *The essentials of imago theory and practice: A paper on basic definitions.* Retrieved from: http://pasadenainstitute.com/d/EssentialsOfImago.pdf

Dass, R. (1971). *Be here now.* Questa, NM: Lama Foundation.

Eastan, P.D. (1960). *Are you my mother?* New York: Random House.

Gibran, K. (1923). *The prophet.* New York: Alfred A. Knopf, Inc.

Gordon, B. (1979). *I'm dancing as fast as I can.* Kingston, RI: Moyer Bell Books.

Hendrix, H., & Hunt, H. (1998). *Giving the love that heals.* New York: Atria Books.

Herman, J. (2015-1R). *Trauma and recovery: The aftermath of violence-from domestic abuse to terror.* New York: Basic Books.

Hudgins, K., & Toscani, F. (Eds.) (2013). *Healing world trauma with the Therapeutic Spiral Model: Psychodramatic stories from the frontlines.* London, Philadelphia: Jessica Kingsley Publishers.

Kushner, H. (1995). *When children ask about God: A guide for parents who don't always have all the answers.* New York: Schocken Press.

Levy, M.S. (1998). A helpful way to conceptualize and understand reenactments. *The Journal of Psychotherapy Practice and Research: 7:227–235.*

Love, P.(1991). *The emotional incest syndrome: What to do when a parent's love rules your life.* New York: Bantam Books.

Maltz, W. (2012 3rd Edition) *The sexual healing journey: A guide for survivors of sexual abuse.* New York: William Morrow Paperbacks.

Mellody, P. (2003, 1989). *Facing codependence: What it is, where it comes from, how it sabotages our lives.* New York: Harper and Row.

Scwhartz, R. (1997). *Internal Family Systems Therapy.* New York: The Guilford Press.

Twelve steps and twelve traditions. (1981). New York: Grapevine, Inc. and Alcoholics Anonymous World Services, Inc.

Whitfield, B. (2011). *Victim to survivor and thriver: Carole's story-hope for survivors of childhood trauma, abuse or neglect.* Atlanta: Muse House Press/Pennington.

Winnicott, D.W. (1953). Transitional objects and transitional phenomena: A study of the first not-me obsession. *International Journal of Psychoanalysis: 34(2):89–97.*

ABOUT THE AUTHOR

As a leader in childhood sexual abuse and addiction treatment, Adena Bank Lees has been providing international training, consulting and psychotherapy services for over twenty-five years. Having lived through many years of feeling 'crazy' from this elusive and rarely spoken of sexual abuse, Adena writes *Covert Emotional Incest: The Hidden Sexual Abuse*, to provide relief and hope for those who suffer. Educating the professional community is a second purpose, encouraging further research and raising widespread awareness of CEI.

Adena is a Licensed Clinical Social Worker, Internationally Certified Substance Abuse Counselor, Board Certified Expert in Traumatic Stress®, and a Certified Practitioner of Psychodrama. Her previous book, *12 Healing Steps for Adult Survivors of Childhood Sexual Abuse: A Practical Guide,* is used by psychotherapists world-wide to aid survivors of sexual abuse in their healing process.

Adena currently lives in Tucson, Arizona, with her wife, Diane. She enjoys singing like no one is listening, hiking in the Sonoran Desert, and filling her days with laughter.

For more information on Adena's work, please go to www.adenabanklees.com.

Printed in Great Britain
by Amazon